SPEAK THE F*CK UP

ADVANCE PRAISE FOR STFU

*"Rachel Smith's first book goes beyond narrative non-fiction, it's a brilliant mix of storytelling, letter writing, and actionable wisdom—a ground-breaking fusion of memoir and self-help that promises empowerment to all who read it. Rachel's journey is a testament to resilience and the transformative power of finding your voice, and will no doubt inspire a movement to Speak the F*ck Up."*

Tegan Quin- Singer/Songwriter band Tegan and Sara,
Author of NY Times bestselling book"*High School*"

"Equal parts joyful and harrowing, Rachel Smith takes us on an inspirational journey of self-empowerment. With astonishing vulnerability and insight, Smith revisits some of the toughest moments in her personal and professional life, giving new meaning to the concept of a teachable moment. Laugh, cry and get chills as Smith shares her experience, then summon the courage to find your voice and SPEAK THE F UP."*

Stephanie Savage- Hollywood Screenwriter.
Co-Creator of Gossip Girl

"Rachel Smith, a jewel of a human being, provides women with an engaging guidebook for clear-eyed self-assessment as well as options for self-expression and personal transformation in these challenging times."

David Friend, creative development editor,
Vanity Fair

"An empowering inspirational tale that resonates deeply. Rachel's story is a battle cry for women-and all people- to find and use their authentic voices."

Hesta Prynn, International DJ and
licensed clinical therapist

SPEAK THE F*CK UP

AN INTENSELY VULNERABLE AND ALL-TOO-PERSONAL ACCOUNT OF ALL THE TIMES I FAILED TO SPEAK THE FUCK UP*

*AND WHAT YOU CAN LEARN FROM THAT

RACHEL SMITH

Storytellers Publishing
COLORADO

Storytellers Publishing
An imprint of Journey Institute Press,
a division of 50 in 52 Journey, Inc.
journeyinstitutepress.org

This work depicts actual events in the life of the author as truthfully as recollection permits. All persons within are actual individuals. Some names and characteristics have been changed, some events have been compressed, and some dialogue has been recreated to respect their privacy.

Library of Congress Control Number: 2023952330
Names: Smith, Rachel
Title: Speak The F*ck Up
Description: Colorado: Storytellers Publishing, 2024
Identifiers: ISBN 979-8-9886470-0-3 (hardcover)
Subjects: BISAC
BIOGRAPHY & AUTOBIOGRAPHY / Women |
BUSINESS & ECONOMICS / Women in Business |
SOCIAL SCIENCE / Women's Studies

First Edition

Printed in the United States of America

1 2 3 4 5 21 33 45 66 78

This book was typeset in Babas Neue/ Book Antiqua

Cover design by Jenna Jaeger

To every woman endeavoring to Speak the F*ck Up

CONTENTS

"When we speak, we are afraid our words will not be heard or welcomed. But when we are silent, we are still afraid. So it is better to speak."
-Audre Lorde

"And the scary thing I have noticed is that some people really feel uncomfortable around women who don't hate themselves. So that's why you need to be a little bit brave."
-Mindy Kaling

"It's time to take the masking tape off my mouth. Like, forever."
-Taylor Swift

PREFACE

The title of this book is bold.

It makes a statement.

The same could not always be said about me.

Writing this book not only describes my personal journey of learning how to speak the fuck up—writing this book was a journey itself.

Make no mistake about it. Speaking the fuck up… is fucking hard.

My journey to get there, to do just the thing that is now the title of the book, was messy and traumatizing. It was ugly, awful, and formidable. An almost Sisyphean undertaking.

My journey of learning how to speak the fuck up started when circumstances brought the life I was living to a grinding halt. In the late summer of 2022, my mother was diagnosed with stage 4 cancer and my world stopped.

Being by her side for her battle became the single most important thing I could think to do. My fiancée Jenna and I moved from Denver to Cape Cod and into a house right next to her.

Anyone that has been a primary caretaker for someone that is so sick understands how days become defined by a schedule of appointments and treatments, and in between, so much contemplation of life, of mortality, of the meaning of it all. I existed in a fog of nostalgia and reflection punctuated by sharp, clear spikes of panic and despair.

I was balancing my mom's needs with the demands of running my own business. Despite being constantly busy, the days felt endless. And I worried about everything. I knew I had to channel my anxiety into something, or I would implode.

A year away from turning fifty, I decided to write a book about my life. Despite having a lot of fodder to write about from my personal life, I found myself focusing on the experiences in my professional life.

My professional journey has been nothing short of wild. A rollercoaster ride filled with hairpin turns, soaring highs, crushing lows, and plenty of opportunities for puking.

I started my career in my early twenties in Hollywood, working for one of the most famous film directors in the world. When I moved to New York City, I rose in the ranks to become a global manager for one company and a senior vice president at another.

I have almost exclusively worked for men.

I started writing about all the opportunities that had come to me over the years.

On the surface, it seemed as if I had been incredibly fortunate. Most opportunities came to me fairly effortlessly, garnered from what I had always considered to be an alchemy of luck and serendipity. Until I dug deeper.

When I started to examine the true source of my career opportunities, I realized that they were rarely attained based on things like my talent, skill, or intellect.

I knew, intuitively, that I had those things. But somewhere deep inside of me, I also knew those weren't the things getting me the jobs.

When I had the job, I would always find myself in an "almost, but not quite" position of power.

I felt close to having respect and confirmation of my talents, and also a hundred miles away. I spent most of my career feeling like something was just a little off. I never got to a place where I felt I had made it, where I was valued, and seen, and heard.

The in-vogue phrase for this is having "a seat at the table."

In many circumstances, I more than earned that seat at the table. Sometimes there would even be a very public and celebratory presentation of the seat for me.

But when I sat down, I discovered the seat was at an empty table, in another room.

I felt tricked because I was.

When I started to write about all of this, I began the painful excavation of what I've come to call "the true- truths."

A true-truth is a profound truth that lies buried deep within us, often under layers of other, sort-of truths.

These true-truths are the ones that wake you up at three in the morning, shouting at you to stop burying them behind impostor truths.

True-truths suck.

What my true-truths told me was that much of what had come to me in my life, career-wise, was because of the way I presented myself as a woman in the world. In my twenties and thirties, and most of my forties, I was a single woman, unattached, and therefore potentially attainable. The fact that I was an out-and-proud gay woman did nothing to tamp this impression. And neither did I. Not enough, anyway. I led with my attractiveness and naivete. And I coupled this with a failure to trust my own intuition and a lack of courage or self-esteem to speak the fuck up.

What started as an innocuous memoir of my time working, first in Hollywood and then in New York City for successful and powerful men, became something else when held under my true- truths' light.

When my true-truths made themselves known, both in the wee predawn hours and in the stark light of 1:00 p.m. "I have no place to be" light of day, that's when this book stopped being a memoir and became something else.

This book became a reckoning. A soul-searching excavation, and the start of a journey.

When I started writing everything down, I was shocked at what I uncovered. There was an easily traced common thread through all my stories, and it was undeniable.

And that's when it started to hurt.

Writing this book hurt. Besides telling the stories of my interesting careers, I had to talk about all the times I had let myself be compromised, silenced, and shamed.

The true-truths were beaming their light directly on me, and it became impossible to do anything else with my writing except figure out why the hell I couldn't speak the fuck up.

I had to uncover what had happened that rendered me unable to truly care for myself. I also needed to understand why I couldn't protect myself from disgusting men, injustices, and wrong assumptions. How had I let myself be constantly objectified, or dismissed?

And those things happened all the time.

I began to uncover a pattern that started when I was a young kid, watching my father abuse my mother. It continued through college, when I came out as gay and shared the most intimate, if complex, aspect of my identity.

And it continued through the entirety of my professional career.

While writing, my emotions ranged from pissed off, to depressed, to downright infuriated. Often, my anger was directed at myself.

I demanded an answer to the same question. Over and over again.

Why could I not speak the fuck up?

When I uncovered this true-truth- how I had consistently failed to speak up in nearly every threatening or unjust circumstance in my life, I realized I had allowed the damage to continue, and to repeat.

I wish I could do it all over again.

I would have done it all differently.

But since I cannot, I will focus on what I can do, which is to speak up about it now. And share the journey of how I got here.

It wasn't easy for me, and it won't be easy for anyone.

But believe me when I tell you, it will be worth it.

If I had been brave enough to speak up from the beginning of my career, I might have suffered some lost opportunities. However, I now believe that doing so would have also created new and better opportunities, ultimately serving me more fully.

Now, I want to be part of the change that makes more opportunities possible for women who do find the courage to speak up. I want to be one of the voices altering the perception of what a woman is doing when she speaks up.

Speaking the fuck up does not make you difficult, burdensome, or less than. Speaking the fuck up does not make you unworthy or undesirable. Not to the people who value you for the right reasons and for the right things. The people who see you and respect you and are worth your time.

When I finished writing this book (for the third time), I knew I finally got it right because I felt I was adding my voice to the chorus of women who are smashing the idea that speaking the fuck up is a risk too great to take.

I am speaking the fuck up now, later than I should have and later than I needed to, in hopes you will find the courage and support to do so in real time.

And any loss you suffer by speaking up will be outweighed by what you will gain. In your dignity, your self-respect, and how you matter to the people who matter to you.

You will not be alone if you choose to speak up.

Just as a rising tide lifts all boats, a rising voice lifts all voices.

I owed this to myself then. You owe this to yourself now. We owe this to the women who come after us.

Speak the fuck up. It's worth it.

Onwards.

INTRODUCTION: WHAT IS THIS BOOK?

When the focus of this book changed from just telling stories and into a deeper excavation, a journey to learning how to speak the fuck up, I knew it was no longer a memoir.

So, what is it?

I now think of this book as a travel friend.

My guess is that most women have that one friend who would always be their first choice to take a journey with. This friend is competent and capable but also easygoing and flexible, able to handle surprises, flight delays, or lost luggage.

She is a sagacious, sometimes irreverent, wonderful friend.

When I developed the structure of this book, I realized I was giving myself the tools and support that the perfect travel friend would give to me on any journey to an unknown place.

Each section in each chapter of this book describes a step in my lifelong journey. The travel friend that is this book got me to my destination.

And I believe she will do the same for you.

The Structure of This Book

Each chapter starts with a *story,* followed by a *letter* I wrote to someone in the story. Then there are the *"Hindsights,"* where I articulate, with the help of perspective, distance, and time, my personal lessons. Finally, the

"Onwards" are calls to action, culled from the wisdom gained through experience, that I can now share with you.

Stories

The stories provide context for what is to come. They introduce the situations and the people that ultimately served to move me closer to the journey's end. There are some funny parts and some harrowing parts. Not all stories are about being silenced or compromised. Some are about being celebrated. All the stories are as true as memory will allow.

More about that in a bit.

Letters

After every story is a letter. In most cases, the letter ties directly back to the story and someone in that story. The letters represent the things I wish I'd had the courage to say at the time.

When I was writing this book strictly as a memoir, there were no letters. I was writing down my stories and then just sitting in the pain of the memory and the disappointment in myself for not speaking the fuck up.

Writing the first letter was unplanned and came as a total surprise. It just happened.

One night, after reading back one of my stories, I was so frustrated and angry that I impulsively wrote a letter to the person in the story that had evoked those feelings.

And then I wrote another letter to someone in another story.

Eventually, that was the only thing I wanted to do. Write letter after letter. I couldn't stop.

I felt like I had discovered something major. A trick, a salve, a way to combat past pain. Writing the letters made me feel like I had finally found my voice. After decades of not speaking the fuck up, I found a way to start.

Almost immediately, I felt something move in me. The pent-up pain or disappointment, now coming to the surface in the letter, started to dissipate. I could feel it leaving my body.

Writing the letters was the single most important tool I discovered for finding my voice.

The letters are what really kick-started my journey to speaking the fuck up.

The travel friend that is this book lovingly demands and insists that everyone reading this tries writing some letters. It can change your life.

It doesn't matter that the letters probably won't be written at the time of the events.

My letters, despite expressing the things that I needed to say in the moment, were all written long after the fact. Some letters were written twenty, thirty, even forty years later.

When I wrote each letter, I went right back to the moment. The only way to move past the hurt and anger of my experience was to write a letter to the person who hurt me. This had a "one step backward, one hundred miles forward" sort of result. The effect was powerful and transforming.

It also doesn't matter that I will never send the letters to what I call the "ILRs"—the intended letter recipients. The simple act of writing down what I wish I had the courage to say at the time started to heal me. And *that* is what matters.

The ILRs have their own journey and their own healing to do. Ultimately, the letters aren't about them, or even for them. They are about me; they are for my healing.

One final note about the letters:

Most of the letters are not lovely. They are impulsive and raw. I spat them out through anger or tears. A few letters *are* lovely. They are written to people that did support me and who did see my potential. In these letters, I am speaking the fuck up to say thank you.

Speaking the fuck up can also be about expressing gratitude and appreciation.

Hindsights

Since the acts of letter writing happened long after each event, the letters often brought with them the gift of hindsight. If not exactly "twenty-twenty," the hindsight I now have really brings things into a much sharper, clearer perspective.

A great travel friend remembers where you started on your journey and reminds you of how far you have come.

These are the hindsights that follow each letter. They are personal to me, and specific to the experience I had, but they often illuminate more collective truths. And they bring things back to the present day; they ground me in the lessons I learned from the experiences and the strengths I gained in writing these letters.

The letters start each individual journey of my speaking the fuck up. The hindsights complete them for me. The hindsights are my takeaways that allow me to understand the empowerment, the growth, and the healing that can exist on the other side of a traumatizing experience.

Between the letters and the hindsights, the painful memories- like a wound that was stitched, can now begin to heal.

Onwards

Onwards.

A clear directive, the word evokes *action*. The Onwards in this book are meant to be like your best travel friend, guiding and encouraging you.

Every chapter ends with an Onwards. Where this travel friend of a book takes your hand and tells you what to do. The Onwards are *your* calls to action. If even just a fraction of one or some of my stories resonates with you, the Onwards will move you *onward* in your own journey of speaking the fuck up.

In the Onwards, I suggest ways to recognize, and overcome, the forces that may have kept you from speaking the fuck up in your own life.

Regardless of where you are on your journey, the actions suggested in the Onwards will move you forward.

They may be bullet points, they may be assignments, they may be meditations.

They are all for you.

These Onwards are not meant to be pedantic or preachy. They are meant to extract the commonalities from within my personal experiences and identify the things that most every woman can recognize as a shared experience.

You can read them once or return to them daily. The Onwards are here as a support, a resource, and a guide—in that unique and all-powerful way that only the understanding and empowerment culled from the shared experiences of women can provide.

Onwards!

***A note on the "as true as memory will allow" part:**

I promise you, every word in every story is true.

And if everything were always entirely fair and honest in the world, the truth alone would be all the protection I could ever need in telling my story.

But I'm not sure if it is.

I have dealt with some truly awful, despicable men.

I don't want to get sued. I can't afford it.

I don't know how viable most nondisclosure agreements (NDAs) are these days, but I signed a shit ton of them, and I can't put myself or my family at risk if one of these men decides I am an appropriate receptacle for all their insecurity and rage.

So, I don't name names.

I struggled with this because I know the book might have had more of a "gasp" factor if I had, and it may have stayed truer to the essence of "speaking the fuck up." However, ultimately, I believe that the point of this book is more about *my* journey and healing than it is about the ILRs and the work they still must do.

Despite the unique structure of this book, it is still reliant on my memory. I have recollected events to the best of my knowledge and used pseudonyms and composites for the intended letter recipients. I have also changed the names of supporting characters in some stories.

That's my disclaimer.

Onwards!

PRESENT DAY

I am sitting at the kitchen table with my fiancée, Jenna. We have just returned home after hosting our fourth Speak the F*ck Up event.

We call our events "Letters and Libations," mostly so women know there will be wine.

At every event, I read a story and a letter, and then we guide women through writing their own letters. One of the most moving things I have ever seen is a roomful of women, so focused on writing their letters and finally saying what they needed to say.

If you are reading this and wondering how or why we started a movement around a book before the book was even published, it's a great question. And it has so much to do with the person I am looking at across the table.

Sitting at the kitchen table now, I am watching Jenna read the letters we received at our last event. They will be posted anonymously to our website, where other women can find them.

During the year that I was writing this book, Jenna was my only reader.

Because we had both committed to staying on Cape Cod to be at my mother's side for her cancer battle, we had adjusted our work schedules and had ample time for personal projects. When I decided to write, Jenna was wholly supportive. She read every page of what I thought would be a memoir.

What she could not have anticipated, because I also didn't see it coming, was what an incredibly shitty, pissed-off mood I would be in all the time.

I was already stressed and anxious beyond words with every doctor visit and scan that my mom had. When I started writing my stories, I lost what little control I had over my emotions. It was as if a dam broke. All my anger and rage came rushing out.

I am amazed Jenna didn't leave me during this time.

Instead, in the evenings, she would bring a glass of wine to me in my writing loft and ask me what I wanted for dinner. I would snap at her for interrupting me.

When I finally wrote my first letter, I burst into the bedroom late one night and announced that I had done it. I had learned how to speak up. I told Jenna that instead of just writing my memoir, I was going to write about this. And I was going to call it "Speak the Fuck Up."

You would think that is the book you are holding now.

But it's not.

Because of Jenna.

My very first letter is to her.

Dear Jenna,

I am so grateful for you. For your patience.

I can't imagine what it has been like for you, this last year of living with me.

I have been a mess of emotions and anxiety and stress. I have dug giant holes of self-pity and wallowing, and then lowered myself into them and stayed there.

When I started to write my book, I know I was even more of a nightmare to live with.

But you stayed.

And when I discovered letter writing as a way of healing, you celebrated me. You were endlessly supportive.

I presented the book to you, thinking it was finished, and you read it and celebrated me again.

And then you gave it back to me to read.
You didn't say anything negative. You just told me to read it again. Especially the letters.
Thinking back to this part of the journey, the first rereading of my book, I remember a quote I have always loved. "A breakthrough looks a lot like a breakdown at first.".
I reread my book, especially the letters, and I had a breakdown.
The letters were not an example of me speaking the fuck up. The letters were apologetic and dainty. I was circling around what I really wanted and needed to say, without even coming close to saying it.
I reread the letters, and I felt pathetic.
When I talked to you about this, you agreed I was far from doing the thing that I set out to do. You explained that you didn't say anything because you knew I would get there on my own.
And I did. Finally.
But not before, or until, you helped me.
We are such different women, you and I. Remember when you "discovered" I didn't really have any female friends? You realized that I had spent so much time alone, depending on myself alone, that I had no idea what I was missing by not having a support system of women around me.
You, on the other hand, have a whole handful of best friends. You have weekly meet-ups and lunches with them. You go to happy hour, have a book club, "do life" with them.
You knew what I didn't.
Women coming together will make every woman stronger. And that quote you would say, something like "Behind every successful woman is a tribe of other successful women."
You knew all of this to be true. I did not.
*When you had the idea to host events for our Speak the F*ck Up project, I now know that you had a plan all along. You knew that putting me with other women, women who would also make themselves vulnerable enough and brave enough to start speaking the fuck up, would embolden me. And you were right.*

I rewrote this book during the six months that we hosted our events. Each time I had to read a new story and letter for an event, I rewrote the letter.
The book got stronger. And so did I.
Jenna, you are my hero and my inspiration.
You always speak up. Without fail.
I know because I've talked to your mother. You've always been this way. Through your adolescence, through college, and in your relationships.
When you were an NFL cheerleader, you came out as gay and brought your partner to your end-of-the-year gala event. Even though you were one of the best cheerleaders, you weren't asked back on the team. You lost something dear to you because you spoke up.
And I know you wouldn't change a thing.
It feels right to start this book by saying thank you, to you. I plan to end it this way too.
Some women, like you, have a natural ability to always speak up.
Others, like me, must learn.
Thank you for showing me the way.
Yours, always,
Rachel

HINDSIGHTS

I wrote this first chapter as somewhat of a bonus chapter during a full edit of the book, and it's ironically the last chapter I wrote. Even before this book was published, it had become much more than just a book. It was the impetus for our Speak the F*ck Up movement-something I am incredibly proud of. Sharing some of those experiences and including a letter to the person who made them all possible (and loved me when I was unlovable) felt like exactly the right place to start.

This book is filled with reflections on my past, so it also felt grounding to begin storytelling in the present day.. Most significantly, this story shows just how far I've come in the journey of writing this book.

One of my biggest realizations with this first chapter is just how hard *actually* speaking the fuck up is.

I wrote an entire first draft of this book *thinking* I was speaking the fuck up. I wrote the last sentence, put my pen down, and believed I had not only exercised my voice but exorcised some deep-seated and damaging past traumas.

For the most part, the stories were fine. It was the letters that crushed me. When I read the first draft, I discovered the letters were pandering and meek. They were mealy-mouthed, apologetic, pathetic.

I berated myself for weeks.

What was wrong with me?

The answer is that nothing is wrong with me. I am a woman living and working in a male-dominated world. Speaking the fuck up goes against everything that we, as women, have collectively been told and taught. When I entered the workforce, I was so young and naive. I knew people found me attractive, but I had no sense of myself or who I was. I felt like I was inhabiting a body and a face with which I had no real relationship. I knew that what people were responding to in me, had nothing to do with the real me. I suffered from a lack of self-esteem and self-worth.

A good psychologist would most likely examine my adolescence and early adulthood. They would recognize that my upbringing, and a few significant and terrible events formed my trauma response from an early age.

What I do know is how I behaved. I placated. I apologized for things that had absolutely nothing to do with me. I was so terrified of confrontation that I never did anything that would further aggravate others. The result was that I carried my hurt with me for years, and I never honed the ability to recognize when a person or situation was dangerous for me. These facts—and society's constant shunning of women that are too loud, say too much, make waves, or blow whistles—shaped me and contributed to my shame and silence for almost fifty years.

Rereading the first drafts of this book, I see now that my words, and the letters especially, still came from this silent, wounded place. I was talking about speaking the fuck up, but I had no idea how to actually do it. I didn't even know if I was capable of it. I had failed, and I felt like a fraud.

Jenna was the person who recognized I needed help. The night at dinner when she reached across the table, took my hand, and said what I was so acutely aware of.

"Honey, you really have no idea how to speak up, do you?"

That was a turning point for me on this journey. Here was someone who recognized my struggle to find confidence in my voice and the courage to use it.

When we had our first Speak the F*ck Up event, it became obvious to me that the key to most everything on this journey was for me to find support. To recognize how common the themes of women's experiences are and to commiserate about that. I needed the safe space that our events created, and I needed other women.

This hindsight needs to be stated again.

I needed other women.

This journey was too hard for me to take on my own.

This book you are <u>now</u> holding in your hands is true to its title.

This book exists because Jenna and I made a safe space where women could speak up, and in doing so, I made a space for myself as well. Listening to and celebrating other women's voices set my own voice free.

ONWARDS

As a reminder from the introduction, these Onwards are here to give you something to think about, and if it feels right, to take action and apply to your own life. These Onwards are always suggestions, not obligations. We are all in this together.

Speaking of that...

Ask For Help...If asking for help feels too vulnerable, just listen to other women.

Help comes from other women! I have seen their power in action, and it is remarkable.

These other women can be friends you already know, or strangers that came together because they saw a cool event posted online. They can be women you meet in Zumba class or someone reaching for the same brand of yogurt you like at the supermarket.

Find other women. When you do, talk about your life. When you feel comfortable, share the times when you didn't speak up, or express what you need to say now. I guarantee these women will support you in doing so, and they'll be happy to meet you for coffee or a drink when you do.

If asking for help is too scary, just listen to their stories. Was there a situation when they spoke up? Take comfort and energy from that. Women are doing this all the time, all around you. Listen to their stories. Through active listening, you'll discover common themes and guidance, and feel a sense of solidarity. Find solidarity with other women.

The most amazing resource we have is each other. Start with women. And stay with women. Ask them what makes them feel better, feel stronger, and feel heard.

The very best news is that you have already done this first Onwards, maybe without even knowing it.

You are reading this book! Even if you can't think of another woman to have this type of conversation with, you have found me. I will tell you my stories and how I learned to speak the fuck up.

Find someone that believes in you—that hears your whispers, if not your shouts.

Jenna was the person who believed in me and heard my whispers. And then she helped me turn those whispers into shouts. It just takes one person. Share your story and your struggle with someone you love and tell them you need their support in speaking the fuck up. Ask them to be a place to retreat or return to while you are working up the courage to speak up. Ask them to be patient and gentle because this work is hard.

And if you look and look and can't find anyone, ask God. However you define that word, whatever higher power resonates with you. Ask the universe, or a flowering tree you pass every day on your way to work. Find someone or something you can say "I got this" to, that will say back with assurance, "Yes. You. Do."

PRACTICE MAKES PERFECT.

This is my favorite Onwards, which is why I wrote it in all caps. Like most everything, from figure skating to playing the piano, practice makes perfect. The same is true of speaking the fuck up. Try it in tiny doses. Try it when the stakes are low. I'm not talking about yelling at someone that doesn't hold the door open behind them (although I hate that), but just practice speaking the fuck up. In a meeting at work, on a date, or to a friend that never asks how you are doing. Say something. Put yourself first and see what happens.

And don't get discouraged if at first your voice is not loud, or strong, or sure. Keep speaking the fuck up.

It gets better and it gets easier. Practice makes perfect.

THE BEGINNINGS—"JUST SOMEONE TO LAY DOWN BESIDE ME"

I won't dwell too much on my childhood. Sharing a story or two should provide a good sense of the kind of kid I was. Truth is, I didn't change much from my early years through boarding school, college, and into my first job in Los Angeles. I was always the same—a chronic overthinker and worrier from the moment I was born.

I am an only child and I carry the triple virgo label in astrology. For those who follow such things, it's often a cause for great alarm. Apparently, it's intense.

My defining characteristic is an unrelenting pursuit and discovery of things to worry about, leading to near-crippling anxiety.

Good times.

Furthermore, I grew up in a house that was filled with chaos: constant shouting, fighting, and nearly just as constant partying.

I learned early on that I needed a safe space. In such a chaotic environment, I was seeking a sanctuary. I realized at five years old that this sanctuary was going to have to be me.

There I am. Bowl-cut bangs almost over my eyes, sitting alone on the floor in the corner of my room. All around me are books, and right next to me is my most prized possession-a blue-and-white-checked record player. I dusted it off every morning before school. I was constantly lifting the arm and examining the needle to make sure it still worked.

On this record player, I would play two records on repeat. The same two songs, for hours, every day after school. The records were called 45s.

If you are too young to know what a 45 is, it's a smaller record. It is the size of half a record. A 45 only has one or two songs per side. You needed a little plastic contraption to play it on a regular record player. The record player, these two 45s, and the yellow insert that made it possible to play them were everything to me.

I would alternate the order of my two favorite songs, depending on the day. Rita Coolidge's "Your Love Is Lifting Me Higher" and Linda Ronstadt's "Someone to Lay Down beside Me."

The first song choice made sense. I *did* want love to lift me higher, higher than I had ever been lifted before! And I was thrilled to have Rita Coolidge to do it. Rita was like my smart, pretty aunt. I imagined she always had candy and that she smelled like sunshine.

One day, my relationship with Rita took a devastating turn. I accidentally found my dad's *Playboy* collection under his mattress. On one of the covers was none other than my Rita. "How could she do this?" I cried to myself.

I wasn't even sure what she "did," but I knew it couldn't be good. Why else would my dad be hiding it under his mattress?

From that day forward, Rita's love did *not* lift me higher.

The second song pick is a lot more confounding. I was seven years old, and I was obsessed with the song "Someone to Lay Down beside Me."

Linda Ronstadt sings woefully about a woman who is so depressed and lonely that she walks the streets at night. She is looking for someone to lay down beside her, and "even though it's not real," it's the story of her life.

This was my favorite song. I sang every word. I felt *every* word.

True to my role as the world's most committed worrier, I worried constantly about Rita and her poor decision-making *and* about the lonely, loose woman in Linda's song.

My love for nakedly emotional (or just naked) female singers, and the near-panic-level state of anxiety I lived in every single day, defined my childhood.

My particular brand of worry extended beyond the typical things kids fret about, like catching an incurable disease or being kidnapped by a clown in a white van. I worried *for the world.*

My parents were known to throw lavish, drug-fueled dinner parties nearly every weekend, and, oddly, my strange affectation toward panic became a part of the evening's entertainment. I was always sent to bed before the mounds of cocaine were placed on the glass-topped dining table, but not before I made "my speech," as my mother called it.

After dessert was served, I would ask for everyone's attention to be directed toward . . . me.

I had pulled out my step stool and would stand on it at the head of the dining room table, next to the wall where the light switches were. From there, I would explain to the guests that the world was at *severe* risk of running out of electricity. "Any day now!" I would whimper-shout. And then, with a shaking, sweaty hand on the round light switch, I would explain that we had what were called "dimmer lights," but if the knob was just turned all the way down and not pressed off (at this point I would demonstrate by pressing off the lights), they would still be emitting electricity. I would ask a dinner guest to come up and demonstrate how to properly turn off the light.

Once I was confident that the electricity message was received, I would move on to the issue of the apocalyptic drought we were about to experience. I would beg the dinner guests to promise me they would not let the bathroom sink drip after they washed their hands.

I would eventually put myself to bed, where I would lie awake for hours, convinced there were dripping faucets and slight-electricity-emitting dimmer lights happening downstairs and bringing about the end of the world. And it would all be my fault.

Years later, a cavalry of therapists would explain that I was looking for stability in my unstable environment. Going to meetings for children of alcoholics, called Al-Anon, would also help me understand I was trying to exert control where there was none. Since I didn't have any control over my day-to-day reality, and chaos, rage, and violence were always just one vodka gimlet away, I tried to control everything else. But at the same time, I was terrified of confrontation. I never wanted to upset anybody, need anything, or be the cause of anything that could threaten the fragility of every day. I was the ultimate appeaser, and I tried to fix everything.

At seven years old, I assumed the role of caretaker. I would hold my mother, crumpled on the floor of the bathroom, as she sobbed uncontrollably about my father abusing her. A few years later, when they separated, I would tell her she was the "most beautiful woman in the world" as she got herself ready to go on a date with my tennis coach, my teacher, or the guy that delivered pizza. And I would order pizza, so there would be something for her to eat when she got home.

On Wednesday nights, when I stayed at my dad's apartment, I would arrive from school and clean his house. I would make his bed, take out the trash, and wait for him to come home.

At about eight o'clock, starving, I would call the Cold Spring Club, where the bartender, Ronnie, would shout over to my father that it was Wednesday night and time for him to go home.

Ronnie would send my dad home with a plate of food, and once my dad ate, I would finish what was left. If I was there on a weekend, I would play hostess to my dad and whatever date he brought home. Mixing cocktails and making cheese plates. One morning I woke up to three women leaving his bedroom.

My parents were dealing with their failed marriage and their rage toward each other by acting out. My dad with drugs and drink and women, and my mom with men. Many, many men.

The one thing they were not doing was paying any attention to me.

When I was twelve, a judge ordered me to go to boarding school. As part of my parents' divorce proceedings, I was asked to share with the judge what had happened during one of their intense fights. The judge asked if I had witnessed my father hitting my mother with a tennis racket, resulting in her jaw being dislocated. The truth was that I had. I had run into a hallway closet to hide when I heard my father coming up the stairs. He was screaming at my mother, calling her a slut and a whore, and shouting that the entire town knew she was sleeping with my (insert current amour's profession here). The fight escalated so much that he picked up the tennis racket and hit her square across the face.

When the judge asked me, point blank, what I had seen, I started to cry. I was twelve years old and felt in that moment that if I told on my father, I would be responsible for him losing his dental practice and potentially going to jail. I told the judge I hadn't seen anything.

Being asked this question in the judge's chambers was the first time I can clearly remember not speaking the fuck up and remaining silent. But how could I? The stakes were just too high. As an adult, I can see so clearly that I should never have been put in that position. My failure to speak up in those chambers changed the course of my next four years.

I am positive the judge knew I was lying. However, without my testimony, there was nothing he could do about my mother's claims. What he did instead was call them both into the room and tell them he was not going to grant custody to either of them. As a result, the decision was made to send me to boarding school.

I know now that all of this broke my mother's heart. I know she felt like I betrayed her by not telling the truth. My mother was devoted to me, and I knew I was her whole world. But she was also consumed with finding validation in her sexual relationships with men, and I hated watching her give herself away so easily. I was angry with her. And I was afraid of losing my dad.

My father didn't remember his own name by seven o'clock every evening, so ultimately it was the right decision for me to go away. The boarding school I attended was half an hour from where I grew up. Most of the kids from my town were day students, but I had to live on campus. I packed one giant suitcase and moved in a week before I turned thirteen.

I was so young-too young. What I needed most in the world was a place where I felt safe. I also needed not to worry every moment of every day.

Dear Dad,

I'm already crying and I haven't even said anything yet. Why are you the hardest one for me?

My entire life, I have felt totally powerless when it comes to you.

Nine out of ten of my childhood memories with you involve you being in a drugged or drunken rage, and me fearing for my life.

I remember the times you would hit me and leave me crumpled and crying in a pile on the floor. I remember running down the street from grandma's house and you trying to run me over with your car.

And I remember the time I have never before been able to speak about. When you came home from the bar one night so wasted that you started to molest me, thinking I was one of your many dates. I still don't know what would have happened if your friend Ronnie hadn't followed you home because he was so worried about you (or me). He threw you off me and punched you into sobriety.

But then there was the one out of ten times.

You would take me fishing on the pier and teach me how to bait a hook. You would carry me in your arms and sing the Moody Blues, all dramatic like you were on stage with the band.

For so long, these were the only memories I would let

myself remember.
I am such a daddy's girl.
I held on to every good memory I had with you. Fiercely.
But you need to hear me now when I tell you, that was one out of ten times.
The other times-you hurt me, constantly.
I always justified everything that you did by telling myself that you were drunk. You were always drunk. I made that excuse for you every single time you hurt me. I told myself it wasn't really you. Not the real you. I told myself that you wouldn't have done any of those things if you were in your right mind.
The most maddening thing of all is that now, forty years later, I know you don't remember any of it.
But I owe it to myself to remember those times.
It hurts me to think of you being hurt when you read this.
But I have to start thinking about myself.
I must start honoring my healing.
And unlike you, I must stop forgetting.
Daddy, I love you. And I have forgiven you.
But I can't keep forgetting with you. For you.
I am grateful that with your older age, you have mellowed, and even though you still drink every day, you don't have the same rage in you.
I think you wore yourself out.
You are not rageful anymore. Now, you are just old.
And now, you call me, every single night at 5:00 p.m., to tell me you love me.
And I tell you right back.
I know that since your wife died, I am all you have in the whole world.
I know that when your health fails, I will be there to take care of you.
Whatever you need, I will do for you.
I think this is why I'm crying.
I am a really good daughter.
I am a great daughter.
You don't deserve to have the best of me, but you have the best of me.

That is just who I am.
But I am done with forgetting.
I finally need to speak about it.
And you need to hear it.
This is the big girl in me, taking care of the little girl in me.
Finally.
I am sending this letter on behalf of that little girl that needed so much more, that was so hurt by you.
My life could have gone in so many different directions.
I could have become an addict, like you, or been destined to stay in abusive relationships my entire life.
But not only am I good, I am held. Something is looking out for me because I didn't do either.
I thrived. Despite growing up with you.
And you don't get to take credit for who I've become.
That belongs to me.
I will talk to you tomorrow at five, and the next day, and the next.
I love you.
But now, I also remember.
Rachel

HINDSIGHTS

Even though it comes at the beginning of this book, this was the last letter I wrote. This letter to my father was, by far, the hardest one for me to write because it is the closest to my heart, at the core of who I am. What I now see in reading it again, the hindsight I have gained, is just how messy the act of speaking the fuck up can be. It can be internally conflicting, contradictory, and all over the place.

In the case of speaking the fuck up to my father, someone I love *so* much—all these things are true. My hindsight is to recognize that this messiness is okay. Not only is it okay, but it makes sense.

I remember when the judge asked me what I saw. I couldn't speak up because it would hurt my father. I made that decision when I was twelve, and I have had to come to terms with it. Love can be the thing that overrides dichotomies of "right" or "wrong." In that moment, love silenced me. This can still happen on this journey. This *will* still happen on this journey.

My work is to find peace with all of it. To have a deeper understanding of when and how I find my voice. And if, at the end of this, I still have limitations, that is okay.

My hindsight is that family, the people you love, will have intricacies attached to your relationship with them, that you may never be able to fully understand.

This is why it is so important to have *different* ways of speaking the fuck up.

It felt so important to write the letter to my father, and writing it felt liberating.

For now, that is enough.

When the book comes out, I will have another journey when he reads it.

One step at a time.

This was an intense letter to start with, but if I didn't write it, I would never get to the real "true- truth" of anything. This letter is necessary, and it sets the tone for everything else.

When I write the stories, I write from my head, trying to be concise but thorough. I write the letters from my heart. They come rushing out, and they are what they are. There is less thinking and more pure feeling.

My final hindsight from this letter is that the healing that comes from speaking the fuck up has nothing to do with the actual words and everything to do with the act. This letter came from the deepest place in me. The words are messy, and they contradict my behavior. But I said it, if only to myself. I spoke up. I am going to be gentle with myself and know that this was a huge first step.

ONWARDS

Step 1: Write a letter to a family member.

Even just seeing this Onwards on the page makes me stop in my tracks. Just as it was for me, you may find this the hardest Onwards and call to action in this book. It is so hard. However, that's also what signals to me how important it is. Everyone has a family, whether you interact with them or not. I know there is a letter inside every woman to someone in her family.

Maybe it's because "we can't choose our family," and maybe it's because these are the first and the longest relationships we can possibly have in this lifetime. This is such an important Onwards. Write the letter-to your father, your mother, your brother or daughter or uncle. Whoever it is that you need to speak the fuck up to.

But before you do, read the next two steps. This Onwards is a three-step process.

Step 2: Recognize the lifetime of dynamics and potential pain this will uncover.

Before you write the letter, take some big, deep breaths, and make sure you are in a safe and nurturing space without many obligations on the other side of the letter writing. Stuff will come up and shit will get real. Throughout writing this book, I had to start and stop so many times. I needed to exercise tremendous patience with myself and summon larger-than-I-was-comfortable-with doses of self-love. You will need to do the same. Just remember, you are not alone. Everyone has a family, and someone out there knows what you went through.

Step 3: Cut yourself some slack and don't judge a word of it.

Not one word. As evidenced in the letter to my father, I may be the world's biggest hypocrite for holding so much pent-up anger and hurt yet acting in a way that looks entirely different. And that is okay.

When I read my letter, I can feel ten-year-old me. I can hear her in the words. The letter isn't elegant or eloquent. But it is what I needed to say. When you write your letter, cut yourself some slack and don't judge a word of it.

Stay within view of your comfort zone.

Most of these Onwards will suggest you do things that put you outside your comfort zone. And that is a great thing. But stay within view of it. You can always go back there. You can always skip any Onward and try again another time.

When I reread this chapter, I recognize that it would make sense and would be important for me to write a letter to my mother. I also recognize I am emotionally unable to do this right now. My mom is in the fight of her life, for her life, and all my attention when it comes to her is on supporting her through this time. I am making the choice not to look backward right now, only forward, for as long as we have left together.

There are no rules when it comes to speaking the fuck up. Listen to your heart and only do what you can, as you can.

DIVISION ONE ATHLETICS—THE REQUEST TO REMAIN SILENT

The boarding school I attended was a mid-level boarding school in New England. Although properly elite, it was not on par with the top-tier boarding schools in the area. It was no Phillips Exeter Academy, for instance, the setting for the novel *A Separate Peace*. Still, many of my classmates came from wealthy families in New York City. These kids were used to having anything they wanted. They summered in Greece and skied in Aspen in the winter. They also hadn't had a sit-down meal with a parent in years. Many of them were closer to their nannies than their mothers.

This was all unfamiliar to me.

I had no idea how to fit into this social network.

I managed to endear myself to some upper-class girls that took pity on me. They took me under their wing and treated me like their sweet, albeit needy, little sister. They were my friends and I thought about them constantly.

When I finally went through puberty, I began to understand that these friendships were actually crushes. I was just starting to realize that I was gay. These older girls, with names like Brie, Autumn, and Fern, could do no wrong in my eyes. They were elegant, glamorous ,and as cool as could be.

Besides the initial discovery of my burgeoning sexuality, the other major happening at boarding school was that I thrived.

I thrilled to the upper-crust boarding school culture of strict rules, curfews, and study hall.

Having grown up without any discipline or the security of meals at a certain time, I loved the structure of boarding school. I had been given a schedule that was calculated to the minute, every day. I was in a personal, orderly, utopia. My little Virgo heart couldn't take it.

I continued to excel throughout my four years of high school. I played three sports and was a tri-captain my senior year. That same year, I was awarded the school's top prize, known as "The Hamilton Webster Thayer Award for Excellence." My grades were excellent, but my ability to follow the rules was unrivaled.

To this day, I love rules, and I love following them because they make me feel safe.

Not only did I avoid coloring outside the lines, I made the lines thicker. I wanted to ensure I stayed *well* inside of them.

That's why what happened next was so interesting.

It seems the only thing that could trump my love of following rules and doing what was expected of me was falling in love.

I graduated from boarding school at the top of my class. Everyone in my life, from my mom to my friends and teachers, was sure I would go to an Ivy League college.

I wasn't as sure.

After I came out as gay my senior year, I started feeling differently about my boarding school.

What had felt like safety now felt too sheltering.

We didn't study books by gay authors. There was no gay-straight alliance group.

I couldn't find any other signs of gay culture anywhere. I was it.

I worried that going to an Ivy League school, most likely in New England, would be more of the same.

From the beginning, I was comfortable with being gay. It made sense to me.

The last thing I wanted to do, as an out loud and proud teenager, was to quiet that.

Whether I was right or wrong about the level of acceptance at an Ivy League school didn't matter. I was claiming my identity, and my choice of college was part of that.

My decision on where to go to college had a lot to do with my ability to claim my sexuality and live my life out loud.

In this book about speaking the fuck up, it is the one place I can say I was unwavering.

I never felt shame or the need to hide the fact that I was gay. From the moment I fell in love with a girl, being gay became one of my favorite things about myself. As many coming out stories do, mine started at summer camp. I was sixteen and feeling myself. Add in a huge dose of "first time falling in love," and my destiny was set.

It was an Olympic training camp for field hockey. The "Olympic" part meant that the camp attendees would be coached by past and future Olympic athletes.

The selling point for attending this camp was that as a high school player, you would be honing your skills with the best of the best. There was a qualifying selection process for attendees as well. Only the top players from high schools were invited to attend.

The only other prospect I had for this summer before my senior year was busing tables at the Beehive Tavern. I chose to go to camp. I knew it was the right decision when I walked into the dining hall the first morning and saw the coaches. I was immediately taken with the group of them. They were the strongest, fittest, coolest, and most confident group of women I had ever seen.

And then I saw her.

Her name was Kat. She had short, spiky, bleach-blond hair. Whispers among the campers confirmed that she was the best national team player at the camp and would be the star of the Olympic team in two years.

I soon learned that Kat was a rule breaker. Instead of walking to the practice field, Kat would skateboard. One day, as I was walking to the field, I watched as Kat sailed by on her skateboard. A UPS truck drove slowly by. In the blink of an eye, Kat kicked up speed and grabbed onto the back of the truck. She rode the UPS truck the rest of the way.

As she passed our group, she gave us a victorious one-finger wave.

It got no cooler than this in my sixteen-year-old brain.

I was smitten.

My focus at camp was now single-minded. I orchestrated my every move to try to put myself in the same place as her. I couldn't have cared less about field hockey. I just wanted to catch a glimpse of Kat.

The night before the final day of camp, Kat performed in the talent show. She did the "Tell Me More" duet from *Grease*. Kat played Danny. She slicked her hair, cuffed her jeans, and rolled a pack of cigarettes into her T-shirt.

Of course she did.

To me, Kat was tanned, toned, perfection.

It really was love at first sight. The reason coming out stories are so powerful is that they are often stories of falling in love *and* discovering your identity. All at once. This is what it was for me with Kat, and it felt powerful.

The final day of camp was the "All-Star" game. The top campers were selected to play in a game against the national team coaches. I was the goalie picked to play in this final game.

I remember *nothing* about the game.

I am certain that I got into the goal, closed my eyes, and didn't open them until the final buzzer.

I would have asked a teammate "What happened?" if I could find one. Instead, when I opened my eyes, all the national team players were racing toward me.

Everyone was shouting and jumping around me, shaking me, and congratulating me. It turns out I had saved something like ninety-two shots in my slumber. I had played an outstanding game. I don't remember any of this.

What I do remember is what happened next. Like a scene from a romantic comedy, the crowds parted and all I saw was Kat. This time, she was running over to me, pushing other players out of the way.

I had never spoken to Kat before. I had never been within five feet of her. This was a lot to take in. Kat was standing in front of me with both hands on my shoulders. She was shouting at me. "That was FUCKING AMAZING. You are amazing!"

The entirety of my energy was focused on trying not to pass out.

Kat went on. "I am going to call my coaches, today! You are *going* to my school!"

Kat didn't pose this as a question or an invitation. Kat was stating this as fact.

I finally caught my breath. After far too many seconds, I stammered a meek, "okay."

And then one more word. The one that would turn out to be key.

"Where?" I asked.

Kat stepped back. With her hands still on my shoulders and with more pride than I have ever seen, Kat said, "The University . . . of Iowa."

I went home from camp that summer and announced that my plans had changed. I told everyone I would be attending the University of Iowa.

My senior year of high school was a blur. I was attending my last year of boarding school in body only. My mind and my heart were already in Iowa with Kat.

We had spent the rest of the summer writing letters back and forth to each other. Kat always signed hers with a #7, her jersey number, after her name.

We decided I would be #6. She said this was so I could be close to her.

What started as innocent quickly turned romantic. By the end of the summer, our letters were mapping out our entire lives together.

I stopped caring about anything but getting to the University of Iowa to be with Kat.

I had a great final season of field hockey that fall. Other college coaches took notice.

I was being scouted at my games by coaches from many other universities.

A disproportionate number of them were named Pam.

One of these was Pam, from Princeton.

She made a really strong case for my going to Princeton instead of Iowa.

Pam said that my combination of athletic ability and

an excellent academic record was exactly what Princeton wanted.

This was my mother's dream come true.

But it wasn't mine.

I agreed to go on recruiting trips to both Princeton and Iowa. In my heart, the decision was already made.

I turned down early acceptance to Princeton.

The day before Christmas break, I informed the Iowa coaches that I would attend their school in the fall.

The decision shocked everyone in my life. I, on the other hand, felt incredibly calm and peaceful.

I was following my heart and claiming my identity. And Iowa was offering me a full scholarship.

College was going to cost me nothing.

I spoke up for what I wanted, and I felt empowered and emboldened. I couldn't wait to start my life with Kat . . . in Iowa.

In February of my senior year, I went there on my recruiting trip. Since I had already stated my intention, it was more of a formality and a welcome.

As fate or young love would have it, a week before I was scheduled to fly out, Kat dumped me. She called me to tell me she was very sorry, but she was back together with her ex-girlfriend. Kat's ex was another player on the team. I was devastated.

When I arrived in Iowa, things went from bad to worse. For dinner the first night, the coaches took me to a steak house for dinner. I was a vegetarian. While I ate iceberg lettuce, the coaches gave me the itinerary for the weekend. They told me that Kat was my assigned guide for the weekend. After all, she was the one that had introduced them to me.

The next three days were something out of a gay horror film. Kat and I had to pretend to be okay while she showed me around town. We went to a bar to meet the rest of the team. Kat's new (old) girlfriend kept giving me the look of death across the bar.

To add insult to injury, a junior-year player named Kelly pulled me aside on the way to the bathroom. Kelly said she needed to tell me that the best thing about going to Iowa was that there were no 'fucking dykes' on the team. It became clear to me that Kat and her girlfriend were not out loud and proud.

I finally got back to my hotel room at two in the morning. Moments after I walked in, the phone rang. It was the graduate assistant coach. She had been hitting on me, subtly, all night. She asked if she could come upstairs.

I woke up the next day to a massive hangover and the coach asleep in my bed.

There was not a doubt in my mind. College was going to be a mess.

It was too late to turn back. I had signed my scholarship letter and I was committed to going to Iowa.

After a brutal week of preseason training, it was decided that I would redshirt my freshman year. This would allow me to have four years of eligibility left to play. Kat's girlfriend was the starting goalie, and she would be graduating the next year. The backup goalie was also an All-American player. I still had to train and practice, but I would not be playing my first year. The irony is that I finished my undergraduate courses in two years. I took electives for one more year, but still got out of Iowa as fast as I could.

And I was right about what a mess it would be.

Since there was no possibility I could play in a game, I decided to break the team rule of no additional exercise on the weekends. I joined a local flag football league. I couldn't have cared less about playing flag football. Instead, I was hopeful I might meet other gay women at the game. If I was going to find any lesbians in Iowa, a flag football game felt like a good place to look.

The Sunday game was just what I needed. As I'd suspected, most of the women playing were gay. They were all older, most of them blue-collar workers at the university or in town. I was so grateful to find women that weren't in the closet or hiding who they were.

When I went to practice on Monday, the head coach asked me to stay after. My goalie coach joined us on the bleachers after the rest of the team had left.

I sat between the two of them while the head coach told me she had received a surprising phone call over the weekend.

Someone had seen me at the flag football game.

I immediately started to apologize. I thought I was in trouble for engaging in physical activity outside of practice or games. I started to ask if that rule applied to me since I was redshirting that year. And then I realized that this meeting was about something else.

The head coach told me I needed to quit the flag football team. She told me I couldn't hang out with any of the other players on that team. After beating around the bush for a few more minutes, the coach got to her point. She told me I needed to not appear gay. The coach told me it would be better for everyone if I kept that part of me "hidden."

I felt dizzy. I focused on the tight curls of her hair. The coach went on to tell me that both of them knew what had happened with Kat. She explained that Kat and her girlfriend were the stars of the team. She couldn't risk anything jeopardizing their season. The coach pointed out that Kat and her girlfriend had made the decision to keep their relationship quiet, and it had served them well.

There was an implicit threat to her words. I didn't know what it could be, but I felt it. It was an open secret that the head coach lived with her partner, Sue. Sue was the team photographer and would come with us on away games. No one ever asked questions.

I started to ask how she could ask this of me when she herself was gay. The coach stopped me before I could finish. She told me to remember that I was on a full scholarship that had to be renewed every year.

I felt totally alone. It was in that moment that I stopped seeing my coaches as role models or protectors. I never again felt that they had my best interest at heart.

I never went to flag football again. Some of the players from that team would come to my games. They held up hand-painted signs with my name and number. I am not sure if any of them knew there wasn't a chance I would get off the bench. I remember worrying that my coaches would see the signs. If one of the flag football players called my name, I would shrink into my goalie padding. What should have been an adorable display of support, terrified me.

College: Part Two

There is no easy way to tell the next part of this story.

As instructed, I remained "quiet" about my sexuality throughout my freshman year.

Off-season, I dated a player on the Northwestern team. On weekends, I would go to Chicago to visit her. I kept that quiet as well.

In the spring, when we were out of training and free of our strict curfew, I went to a party with the rest of my team.

It was a party at one of the star wrestlers' houses. He was dating Emily, one of my field hockey captains.

The two best teams at Iowa were the women's field hockey team and the men's wrestling team. What you must understand about where and when I went to school is this:

Iowa doesn't have any professional sports teams.

If the field hockey players were the pretty princesses, the wrestlers were kings.

They had won twenty-one national championships and during this reign, the entire state of Iowa worshipped them.

A lot of my teammates dated wrestlers, and the only parties we all went to as a team were wrestling parties.

From the moment I walked into the party, I was uncomfortable. I worked my way through the crowd and onto a small balcony.

I was soon joined by a man whom I recognized as one of the assistant wrestling coaches. He was much older than the rest of the guys on the team. I knew about him because he had won a gold medal at the Olympics before returning to Iowa to coach.

On the porch that evening, he told me how he had watched me for the whole season. He said he was always impressed with my work ethic and how hard I pushed myself in the weight room. The wrestling coach commented that I always seemed to be in a good mood. He said he liked how I didn't seem easily swayed by what my teammates were doing.

I couldn't understand his interest in me. Not only was I not a star player, but because I was redshirted, I hadn't even played in a game. For a split second, I wondered if maybe he too was gay. I thought that perhaps his interest and kindness were his secret way of telling me.

I didn't really think this was the case, but I softened.

I graciously took his compliments and thanked him for coming over to talk to me.

Eventually, I found a way to excuse myself and asked for a ride home with our designated driver. Five of us piled into the assistant coach's car. She dropped everyone off at their apartments nearby.

Since I lived in the freshman dorms further away on campus, I was the last to be dropped off.

When I unlocked the door to my dorm room, the wrestling coach was sitting on the edge of my bed.

His demeanor had completely changed.

He briefly explained that he had found out where I lived and drove over. He said he wanted to continue the conversation we had started.

What I didn't know at the time was that upon arriving at my dorm room, he told my roommate I had invited him over from the party and that I was just behind him in a teammate's car.

He told her I had instructed him to wait for me in my room.

My roommate, Megan, didn't find any of this suspicious. She recognized him from the wrestling team and knew I had gone to the wrestler's party. She had been dating a baseball player since preseason and hadn't gone to this particular party.

Upon hearing this story, Megan let the wrestling coach in and went upstairs to stay with her boyfriend, Billy.

In my room, I started to tell the wrestling coach I was feeling very uncomfortable, and that I just wanted to go to bed.

He didn't hear me.

Within seconds, he was on top of me.

I remember crying and pleading with him to stop, but he didn't.

He was mumbling under his breath, while he raped me and took my virginity, that he was going to "convert me."

Later, this phrase would come up again. A teammate relayed to me that she had heard he was telling other wrestlers on the team that he had indeed converted me, and that I was no longer gay.

I was too traumatized at the time to understand what was happening.

Beyond the act itself, this man was talking openly about raping me.

He was bragging about his conquest, and how he had changed my sexuality.

He was talking about it.

I, on the other hand, was too afraid to say anything, for fear of my life.

I knew that speaking the fuck up about what happened that night would, at best, ostracize me from anything and everyone I had forged a connection with, and at worst, it would jeopardize my physical safety.

There is no way that my coaches didn't find out what happened to me.

The athletic community was too small, and the wrestling team was too big, for this not to have gone beyond locker room gossip.

No one ever said anything to me.

About two weeks after the rape, we were scheduled for team therapy.

This was something the team opted to do after a player at a competitor school had committed suicide months before. This was the 1990s, and things were different for female athletes. I knew the woman, and I believe she was in con flict over her sexuality and was hiding the fact that she was gay in a hostile environment, but I cannot be entirely sure.

Following this incident, the entire team was asked to meet with a psychologist to discuss anything that might be bothering us.

At team therapy, I did not talk about the rape.

I did however announce, to the entire team, that I was gay. I was just over all of it. All the pretending. Something in me had been both broken, and broken free.

Most of my team was supportive. They all told me they knew already.

One woman, named Stacy, told me she really liked me and was going to do her best to understand this news. She asked me to also try to understand her, and how this news would be hard for her. She explained that she "was from New Jersey, and there weren't any gay people in New Jersey."

That is a verbatim statement. Stacy honestly believed there were no gay people in the entire state of New Jersey.

Interestingly, many years later, quite a few of my teammates have come out.

They have married their partners and are living happy and healthy lives as gay women.

That wasn't the case in college. Even if they had been gay at the time, they would have been told they couldn't talk about it.

I never heard a word from my coaches about anything that happened my freshman year.

I never made up my redshirted year.

Instead, I graduated in three and a half years and left in December after my final season.

I left the University of Iowa, and I haven't been back in twenty-eight years.

Dear Coaches,

I hated my college experience and being an athlete on your team.

It wasn't the insane workouts you put us through. It wasn't even your yelling at me in front of everyone about what a slow runner I was.

That didn't bother me.

I am a slow runner.
What did bother me was the culture of shame and denial you created for all the gay players on your team. You were also gay! And yet, you made being gay a shameful and forbidden thing on your team.
You gave implicit permission for blatant, and cruel, homophobia.
You willfully ignored all the things that hurt me deeply.
Your silence makes you complicit in everything that I went through.
You made a young, happy, proud woman doubt her identity.
You made me ashamed of who I was.
I arrived at your school with a broken heart. And then, you broke my spirit.
I know you know what happened to me at the end of my freshman year.
It is impossible for me to separate the pain of that event from the pain I felt, every day, being on your team.
I can't help but wonder if maybe that terrible thing wouldn't have happened to me if there was nothing to "convert" me from. If I had been allowed to be myself, to be out, from the beginning.
Maybe that disgusting man would have recognized that I was untouchable.
Maybe the story of my life wouldn't have included a violent rape at the age of eighteen.
I will never know.
You might have chosen to live in secrecy and shame, but by the time I came to Iowa, I did not.
You made me change that.
I don't have a single good memory from college.
Most people can think of at least one or two.
I cannot.
Your cowardice, and lack of courage to do anything that might possibly expose you, put a young woman at risk.
Worse than that, it altered my life forever.
Rachel

Dear Wrestling Coach,

You didn't convert me.
You raped me.
End of story.
Rachel

HINDSIGHTS

It makes me sad that this experience, which happened my freshman year, is the only thing I really remember from college. The next three years were a blur. I have so much deep-seated anger, and I realize it is as much toward my coaches as it was toward the man who raped me. In different ways, and I know this is a bold statement, they both tried to convert me.

I recognize now that had I not been a strong person, my college experience could serve to define me even today. But something was, and has always been, bigger than this trauma.

I love being gay.

Being gay has brought me so much joy. I have learned so much from the women I have dated, and about the world in general. When you move through the world as an "other," you see it differently. I have felt the unwavering support of the LGBTQIA community since I came out.

I love being a part of it, and that love is so much greater than this experience.

The fact that I stayed at Iowa is now also a source of pride for me. I must have strength in me because I didn't let this awful thing beat me. I didn't quit.

I hated every day I was at that school. But I wasn't a quitter. I had committed, and I was going to see it through.

The hardest story brings on the greatest hindsight.

I am strong.

I am strong.

I am strong!

Also, I can say- fuck you. To everyone that was there and complicit in my rape.

I don't have to forgive, and I don't have to forget. I hope word gets back to you and that you are forced to reflect on what you did to a proud young woman.

Venomous, maybe. But this is how I feel. And I am starting to honor that.

ONWARDS

Just because they have the title doesn't mean they deserve your respect.

Have you ever noticed how loaded some words can be? Boss. Leader. Coach.

These words all carry with them this assumed reverence and respect.

But for this Onwards, I ask you to think about someone in your life that has a title like this, and to separate the person from the title. Do they deserve the respect the title automatically gives them?

I was crushed when my coaches, women I looked up to more than any other women in my life at that time, revealed themselves to be hypocrites on such a fundamental level. They were both former Olympic athletes, and they were good "coaches," but as people, I cannot be so sure.

Separate the person from the title and ask yourself if they are people you truly believe in and respect. It's a way of claiming your experience and trusting your intuition. Instead of just allowing societal constructs to demand that you respect someone, look at their actions.

After you do so, even if you continue to train with them or work for them, you will gain a sense of autonomy that will feel empowering. You will make your own decisions about them, rather than just kowtowing to a title.

Reminder: Trauma doesn't have an expiration date.

I wrote this Onwards in the Notes app of my phone late one night during the editing process. I wrote it and fell back to sleep. When I pulled it up the next day, I was struck by how powerful these words were. And I had never heard them before.

Trauma doesn't have an expiration date.

Most everything we consume in the media around trauma is about how "time heals all wounds." But what if it doesn't? And even if we do go on to live happy, healthy, "normal" lives, that doesn't mean that a traumatic experience doesn't still live within us. It might never go away. It might affect us in ways we will never be conscious of.

Which is all to say, honor this.

Be gentle with anything unhealed in yourself because there is no amount of time that can ensure that something will ever disappear from your being completely. The truth, instead, is that it may never leave you. And understanding this, recognizing it, can help you on your journey to finding your voice.

The first person we must speak up to, always, will be ourselves. This journey demands examination, not denial.

I know this is difficult to think about, but our goal is to move towards more lightness, and to move away from shame.

Find someone to talk to.

I am a fan of therapy. I also recognize that traditional therapy can be expensive, inconvenient, and unrealistic for many. There are other options. There are free support groups, both in real life and virtually.

The internet has made so much more possible, and finding support is one of those things.

This is such an important Onwards because nothing about these calls to action is easy, and they can all be incredibly triggering. It is so important to have a safe space to talk to someone about what comes up for you.

The one good thing I can say about my experience in Iowa was that, after my rape, I found my way to something called RVAP: a rape victim advocacy program with a physical location in Iowa City. I went there, and later I volunteered there. And it was always free. And I believe it was a big part of the reason I could handle what happened to me.

Find someone to talk to.

HEADING WEST—LIGHTING OUT FOR THE (GAY) TERRITORY

The year before I graduated, the state of Iowa failed to pass the Equal Rights Amendment for women. This was no state for me. I already knew that, of course, but this confirmed it.

After three and a half years, I had finished my requirements to graduate. Despite having two more seasons of eligibility on my field hockey scholarship, I got the fuck out of Iowa.

So much of my college experience was about just getting through each day. I hadn't given much thought about what I wanted to do with my life. The only thing I knew for sure was that I was gay. Gay with a capital G-A-Y. And written in neon above me like a Tracy Emin painting. GAY.

Every day at practice, I would have hours in the goal when nothing was happening. I would daydream about a time when I could be with other gay people.

Not only would these people be gay in my daydream, but they also wouldn't be afraid of it. They would be proud to be gay.

The only thing that I was sure I wanted was to not feel ashamed about who I was.

I didn't have anyone to talk to about this fantasy of mine, so I read a lot of books.

My senior year, I found a copy of *Tales of the City* by Armistead Maupin. I devoured the series in record time. These books put the idea of San Francisco in my head.

A flip through a travel guide confirmed that some sections of San Francisco were predominantly gay. I wrote down one place in particular, "the Castro."

In my imagination, San Francisco became a magical place. I pictured it was full of rainbow flags and people dancing in the streets.

On these streets, I envisioned gaggles of gay girls, all there to welcome me. I decided that if I could just get to San Francisco, everything was going to be all right. I let myself fantasize that in San Francisco, things might even be wonderful.

I needed to get to San Francisco immediately after I graduated.

I knew exactly one person in San Francisco. A dentist named Martin Hull.

Martin and my father had gone to dental school together. They started their practices around the same time and became good friends. They also started taking a lot of cocaine together.

There have been studies about dentists who got addicted to cocaine. There was a period when dentists could prescribe it to their patients. Martin and my father made the most of the window of time before cocaine became illegal.

Years later, my dad had substituted massive amounts of cocaine for a steady diet of vodka gimlets, while Martin got completely sober.

By the time I was finishing college, Martin had been sober for almost twenty years. As a result, he always remembered to send me holiday cards.

As I got older, he revealed more of his progressive, liberal viewpoints to me. I felt safe telling Martin I was gay.

I called him and told him about my predicament of being gay in a place like Iowa. I explained that I just had to live in San Francisco, so that I could find my people. I asked him if he could help me.

To this day, I am grateful for Martin. On that call, he told me I should come visit him. He said he would take me to look for apartments, and if I couldn't find a better job, he would hire me as a receptionist in his dental practice.

Things were looking up! I was one step closer to my rainbow-tinged San Francisco dream come true.

I packed up my baby-blue Acura Integra and started driving west. I was headed for my golden destiny in the Golden State. Contradictory to my controlling nature, I didn't have any plan other than to keep heading west. I was twenty-one years old, and I had $1,300 to my name. All I knew was that I was GAY. And at that moment, it felt like enough.

I would drive about fourteen hours a day. My rule was to stop driving just before the sun set. The places where I could afford to stay make me itch to think about now. I don't think I spent more than forty-five dollars on a motel the entire way.

Before I left, I had connected with a gay friend from Provincetown named Lee.

Lee was much older than I was, but she was also trying to make a fresh start. Not wanting to spend another winter in Provincetown, Lee was also "headed west" to pursue her dreams in Hollywood.

I didn't know anything about Los Angeles, but felt no desire to go there. I hadn't read anything in the *Fodor's* guide about it being gay friendly. I only knew what I saw on television, and I didn't see anything there that felt like me.

Lee told me she was house-sitting for a week in LA while she looked for her own place. She said I was welcome to crash there for a few nights on my way up to San Francisco.

The thought of a friendly face and a free place to sleep was enough to make me say yes.

My route was taking me on the 10 Freeway right into the heart of Hollywood. When I saw the green exit sign that said "Hollywood," I wondered if this was the sign everyone was talking about. It seemed anticlimactic to me. And then something took my breath away.

I looked over to the side of the highway and noticed there were flowers.

Not just any flowers, but exotic, colorful flowers. Birds-of-paradise. They were growing right there, on the side of the 10 freeway. I was stunned.

Growing up in New England, I was lucky to see a couple of dandelions at a rest stop. Seeing these flowers on the side of the Los Angeles 10 Freeway seemed extraordinary.

And that was before I noticed the mountains. I was overwhelmed by the beauty of Los Angeles. I drove all the way to the Pacific Ocean, got out of my car, and just stood there with my jaw dropped. The New England Atlantic, with its tiny waves, was the only ocean I knew, and she paled in comparison to this marvel.

If the Atlantic Ocean is the bookish, "pretty behind her glasses" younger sister, the Pacific is the hotter, older sister. The miniskirt-wearing, wine cooler-drinking one at the party, with feathered hair and hoop earrings, that gets everyone's attention. She was my kind of girl.

Even before I got to the house where Lee was staying, I was charmed by Los Angeles.

The complex where the apartment was located had what I now understand to be a very *Melrose Place* vibe, the popular nineties television show.

In actuality, the apartment was only a few blocks north of Melrose on Fairfax avenue.

The dozen or so apartments framed a small courtyard. The courtyard had some flowering trees.

I arrived at the apartment at about six in the evening. The smell of bougainvillea and night-blooming jasmine filled the air. When Lee opened the door to greet me, I must have looked shell-shocked. Between the highway flowers, and the ocean, and now this smell, I was totally enchanted.

The next morning, I woke up and went for a run. I had no idea where I was in the city, so I just started running up Fairfax toward the mountains in front of me. I crossed Sunset and followed some people walking through a gated entrance. I had stumbled onto Runyon Canyon.

Years later, I would know Runyon Canyon as "dog poop park," but not today. On this first day in Los Angeles, Runyon Canyon was the most beautiful place I had ever been. I couldn't believe how much I loved what I was discovering in Los Angeles.

That afternoon, I went for a drive on Sunset, and headed back towards the beach. I put in a mixed tape that started with my favorite song, "Anything, Anything" by Dramarama. I blasted it and sang at the top of my lungs. At a stoplight in Beverly Hills, a cop pulled me over. When I asked if I was speeding, he said no, but that it looked to him like I was having too much fun. I didn't get a ticket.

After an afternoon of exploring Venice and Santa Monica, I started to head back to West Hollywood. I stopped in a little town called Brentwood. I didn't know at the time, but Brentwood is one of the most affluent enclaves in Los Angeles. I remember thinking, "Gosh, this is pretty."

Still on a strict budget, but hungry as could be, I looked around for a place to eat. A bright, hand-painted sign that said "Rio Juice" caught my eye.

Even now, if I can close my eyes, I can remember how Rio Juice smelled. Fresh, pulpy, healthy.

I walked in and that's when I saw her. She was tall, and blonde and Brazilian, I realized when she spoke. Her name was Vanessa.

She owned the juice bar with her dad. They had moved to Los Angeles from Brazil a year ago and opened it. I would soon find out that Vanessa was a surfer and that all she cared about was waves. And weed.

The way you do when you are twenty-one and in a new city, I fell instantly in love.

It was as if my enchantment with Los Angeles had been anthropomorphized.

I probably had four juices that afternoon. Vanessa sat with me and told me stories about epic waves and epic weed. I told her I was passing through on my way to San Francisco.

I went back to where Lee was house-sitting, loaded up my baby-blue Acura, and got on the road.

I was feeling enchanted with what I had discovered in Los Angeles. Vanessa, the Pacific Ocean, night-blooming jasmine. Still, I was determined to make it to the gay mecca that was San Francisco.

Driving into San Francisco was nothing like driving into Los Angeles. I don't recall a single flower on the side of the road.

Martin lived in the heart of the city. It took me an hour to find the address and another forty-five minutes to find parking. And I still had to walk twenty minutes to his apartment.

When he opened the door, Martin could not have been warmer or more welcoming. We had dinner and talked into the evening. The next day, Martin took me on a tour of all the neighborhoods.

We had lunch in Chinatown and visited most of the tourist destinations. Everything was interesting, but nothing felt quite right. I told Martin that I needed to do some exploring on my own. I headed off that night in search of the Castro, the part of town I had heard was gayest of them all.

When I arrived, I found a bit of what I was looking for. There were rainbow flags in the windows of bookstores and coffee shops. I saw plenty of women, but none that I found attractive. At twenty-one years old, I was deeply superficial. My primary motivation for everything was to date beautiful women. They could also be interesting and intelligent, but beautiful and gay were my main criteria. The women I met in San Francisco felt militant. Like they were more interested in revolution than Revlon. I loved their passion; I just didn't feel passion for them.

I was also thinking a lot about Vanessa, highway flowers, and the Pacific Ocean. All back in Los Angeles.

The next day, Martin and I went apartment hunting. We found a studio apartment for rent in the Pacific Heights area of the city. Pacific Heights felt like the opposite of a gay mecca. The apartment was tiny. A counter with a hot pot qualified as the kitchen. The bathroom lacked a door. And the monthly rent was three times my entire life's savings.

Standing in the apartment, I knew right then that I wouldn't be moving to San Francisco. I spent a final night in the city with Martin. I thanked him for his hospitality, and the next morning I drove south, back to Los Angeles.

I felt great about my decision. By the time I got back to Brentwood, I was blasting my favorite song and feeling that sense of freedom I had only found in Los Angeles.

I would soon remember that I was now homeless with very little cash. I was down to just under $500. I filled a parking meter with enough quarters for forty-three minutes and headed back to Rio Juice.

All I could think about was how I had not thought any of this through.

I stuck to my shortsighted plan of having a juice.

At least the juice would be free if Vanessa was working. To my delight, she was. I took my juice outside and turned my face to warm in the Southern California sun. I was still without a plan, but I was feeling good.

I opened my eyes to observe a man sitting across from me on the patio. He was white-haired, clean cut, probably early sixties. He looked out of place in the casual, surfer vibe of Rio Juice.

We smiled at each other. He must have seen me talking to Vanessa because he asked me if I came there often. He seemed safe, and I had nothing better to do, so we struck up a conversation. I told him about my road trip to San Francisco. I explained I thought I would end up there, but I had just decided that I preferred Los Angeles. I told him I was having a juice while I figured it all out.

Nothing about this man felt at all creepy or lascivious. He had a sort of "tired dad" demeanor. He listened to my story and shared a bit about himself. His name was Stephen, and he was a neurosurgeon, based in New York City. He was visiting Los Angeles to check on his elderly parents.

Stephen explained that he had grown up not far from where we were sitting. He said his parents were still living in the same house he grew up in. Stephen shared that while they were in their nineties, they were doing just fine. He said his dad had small episodes of "forgetting things" but that his mother was sharp as a tack. She was just slowing down a bit.

He had one sister, who lived in Ohio and didn't get out there much to visit. Which was why Stephen had made the trip. He would be heading back to New York shortly.

I listened and asked some questions, mostly to pass the time.

And then Stephen had an idea.

What if I moved in with his parents? He got excited and mentioned a guesthouse on the property. He explained his parents were still totally self-sufficient, but that it would be great for him to have someone he could check in with. He said his mother didn't always answer the phone and having someone living there would give him peace of mind.

In exchange for moving into the guesthouse and answering the phone when he called, Stephen told me I could live there rent-free.

I had watched enough of *Beverly Hills, 90210* to know that wealthy people in Los Angeles often had guesthouses, and they were fantastic. They were usually set just behind giant swimming pools. They had sliding glass doors and wood beam ceilings. I could picture it perfectly. And I could picture myself living in one. I couldn't believe my incredible good fortune in figuring out a way to stay in Los Angeles just hours after returning there.

I fantasized about inviting Vanessa over for dinner after work. I would make her a casual but delicious meal of grilled shrimp and salad. I would serve it alfresco by the pool.

Stephen gave me the address and explained that it was no more than half a mile up the road. The address placed the house in Brentwood.

I was sure my imaginings were true. The houses I had seen in Brentwood were all mansions.

Everything was happening so fast. Stephen checked his watch and said he had to catch his flight back to New York. He said he was over the moon that we had figured out this arrangement. I needed a place to live, and he needed to feel good about his parents staying in the house they loved. Stephen said that it was serendipity that we had met.

I know I should have asked more questions, but serendipity was one of my favorite words. I felt like I had nothing to lose.

Stephen was now running late and apologized for being unable to take me to the house himself. He told me he would call his mother from the airport and explain everything. He assured me I would be welcomed with open arms. Stephen shook my hand and told me I should plan on moving in the very next day.

I was elated. I don't remember where I stayed that night, but I could barely sleep. I was going to be living in the guesthouse of a Brentwood mansion!

The next morning, I drove my baby-blue Acura to the address on the napkin Stephen had left with me.

I kept checking the numbers on the house to make sure they matched the ones on the napkin.

When I found the right house, my heart sank. This was no mansion. It looked like a house I could find in Iowa. Made of brick, it was old and run down. The windows had grids of small panes, and there was no front yard or blooming thing in sight.

I was hopeful that the dingy facade belied a beautiful home inside.

When I got closer and peered in the window, I realized this was not the case. The house looked dark and damp. It looked like it hadn't been decorated, or cleaned, since the early 1970's. I walked around the house to discover that instead of a pool, the only backyard was a brick patio with some old, rusted furniture.

Stephen's mother answered the door. She took my hand in both of hers and smiled warmly. At least Stephen had let her know I was coming. My first sense was that she was lovely, but not all there. What I remember most was the beautiful long white braid running down her back. I could imagine she was a stunning woman sixty years ago, when she was young.

We started through the house. She pointed out the kitchen. It was dark and cluttered. The living room was slightly brighter, due to a few lamps scattered about. Sitting in a reclining chair in the living room was Stephen's father. He had fallen asleep watching television.

I remembered that Stephen had said his dad was in his nineties. This man did not look a day younger than a hundred and twenty.

His frail body was curled over in a hook shape. His head was cocked so far to the left, it looked like he would topple over at any moment. His mouth was hanging open. Stephen's mother shouted to him and he briefly shook awake. He made a few grunting sounds and fell asleep again.

We moved on to where I would be living. The guesthouse. This turned out not to be a separate house at all. Instead, it was another dark, damp room situated just off the laundry room. There was orange shag carpeting, a small twin bed, and a bathroom. The shower was missing its door.

There was one window that overlooked the brick backyard.

This was my new home.

I can't recall the emotions I had. I think I may have been numb.

Disappointment flooded through me, but I knew it was my only option. The night before, I had taken Vanessa out for sushi to celebrate and had made a significant dent in my savings.

Both my parents were preoccupied with new marriages. My dad was on his honeymoon on some island, and my mom was MIA. They were also three thousand miles away. I knew two people in Los Angeles, but they weren't people I could ask for help.

I had nowhere else to go.

I decided I would make the best of it. I thanked Stephen's mother for her kindness and hospitality and asked if there was anything I could do for her.

The answer was a resounding yes.

It turned out these two nonagenarians were anything but capable of living on their own. For the next three months, I did everything for them. I shopped for them, cooked their meals, and cleaned up after them. I spent almost all day, every day, caring for them.

I had no rent to pay, but I also wasn't making any money. The woman had an uncanny ability to figure out what her groceries would cost, almost to the penny. When I went shopping, I almost always had exact change. The most I bought myself was a box of Special K, some of which I ate for breakfast every morning.

Soon I had a routine. I would wake up early and make breakfast for both of them. I would make them eggs and toast, while I would have my cereal. I would eat it with a tiny coffee spoon to slow myself down. Breakfast usually took them about forty-five minutes to get through. After breakfast, I would do the dishes, run the laundry, make the beds, and clean the living room.

In the afternoons, I would go to Temescal Canyon. It was a beautiful hike in the Angeles Mountains. I would walk to the same waterfall every day, and once there, I would make a wish for something wonderful to happen in my life. That, or I would wish to somehow come into a lot of money, because I was quickly running out of it.

After my hike, I would go to Gelson's supermarket in the Pacific Palisades. I ate every free sample they had, trying to be surreptitious. I would make a salad from the salad bar, taking care to select only the lightest ingredients, since you paid by weight. My salad bar budget was seven dollars a day. I would eat half of my salad for lunch and take the other half home for dinner.

For three months, this is how I spent every day.

I realized early on in living with him that Stephen's dad was suffering from severe dementia, not bouts of forgetfulness. On bad days, he would scream and shout things that made it clear he believed he was still a fighter pilot in the war.

I tried to get in touch with Stephen almost every day. It usually went straight to voice mail. Any time I got him on the phone, he would tell me he was on his way into surgery, and he would call me back. Our calls were always so quick, I never had the chance to tell him how bad off I felt his parents were. I believe he knew.

I just couldn't understand how a grown man, a doctor, could have possibly fathomed that it was okay to leave a young woman with zero health care experience, in charge of two elderly people in need. Not being paid was one thing. Having almost zero contact with Stephen was an even more egregious reality.

I asked the woman for her daughter's number in Ohio. She just waved her hands and wandered into another room.

At the end of every day, I would collapse onto my twin bed exhausted. I would be falling asleep by nine. My sleep did not last long. The nights were when things got really bad.

Sometime between midnight and one a.m. an awful sound would wake me up. A wailing. The first night I heard it, I thought an animal was being tortured and killed by wild coyotes in the canyons. The sound was so pained. Then I realized it was coming from inside the house.

The first night I entered the man's bedroom, I found him lying on the floor, making the sound. He had fallen out of bed. He had also had an accident. Two accidents. His sheets were stained, and the stench was horrible. And he was covered in it.

This started to happen at least four nights a week. He didn't always fall out of bed, but he would always piss and shit himself and make that awful wailing sound.

I came to have a routine on these nights too. I would carry the man into the bathtub, wash him down, change his sheets, and get him back into bed. I would return to my room at about two in the morning, wash the dirty sheets, and get in the shower. I would finally crawl back into bed at three, only to be up again at six.

It was all too much. I felt totally alone and totally overwhelmed.

I was not prepared, capable, or qualified to take on the situation that confronted me. I wasn't in touch with my parents. Lee was nowhere to be found, and Vanessa moved on after she saw my living situation. I was also now down to less than $300.

I kept trying to get in touch with Stephen. Finally, at the end of March, I left him a voice mail telling him I had to leave. I was exhausted, broke, and desperate. I told him that his father had severe dementia, no control of his bladder or bowels, and was at the end of his life. I said that his mother was in denial, and that I was their only source of care and comfort.

I told Stephen's voice mail that I couldn't do it anymore, that it was just too much.

At the risk of sounding too California New Age, the night before I made this call, I saw my first and only angel. It was after one of these late-night episodes. I was back in my twin bed, lying there staring at the ceiling, when I saw her above me. She was all white and in a flowing dress, floating horizontally over me. She was motioning to me with her arms. She was pushing at the air, telling me to "go." To this day, seeing this angel, as clearly as if it were a living person standing in front of me, is one of the most significant moments of my life. This angel, and her message telling me to leave, changed the trajectory of my life.

Stephen never called me back. One morning soon after my angel visit, I sat with the woman while she finally called her daughter, and they arranged for her to fly out the next day. I have no idea why this option wasn't offered sooner. I never spoke to the daughter directly, but I was relieved and grateful that family would be coming to help. I needed to be free of this responsibility.

Before I left, I made sure the couple had enough food. I finally got in touch with Lee and met her in Studio City, where she lent me $200. Lee had recently found steady employment as a production assistant on a television show.

There was one more thing I wanted to do before I left Los Angeles.

I drove to Venice, found a tattoo shop, and got an angel inked in the center of my upper back. I never thought I would have a tattoo, but this felt important. I wanted to remember the challenging time I had just lived through. I wanted an angel tattoo to remember how one had saved me. I didn't know how tattoos were done and didn't realize I could have brought in a picture of what I wanted, instead of just getting the tattoo artist's interpretation of 'angel'. It didn't matter.

She was *my* angel and she had shown up just in time. And now she was forever with me.

I got in touch with my mother. I told her what had been happening to me. I told her how lost I was and how scared

I was. I told her I had to leave but that I didn't know if I had enough money for gas to drive across the country.

My mom listened to my story and told me she had an idea. She said that if I could just make it to Dallas, she would fly and meet me there, and we could meet up and stay at her brother's house. I didn't know it yet, but my mom was going through her second divorce and needed to get out of town as well.

I had never been to Dallas. I knew my uncle had moved there and was working as an ob-gyn at one of the big hospitals. He was also the quintessential bachelor at the time. He drove a Ferrari and dated more than a handful of the Dallas Cowboys Cheerleaders. I wasn't close to him.

I weighed my options.

Dallas was closer than Cape Cod. I had very little money to my name, and I could really use some family.

I packed up my baby-blue Acura and got myself to Dallas, Texas.

Dear Stephen,

You didn't even have the balls to answer my calls.

The few times we talked, you knew something was very wrong. But you chose to ignore it.

Did you think it would just go away, or are you truly just that awful?

I want you to know that putting an untrained twenty-one-year-old in charge of your two elderly and mentally ill parents was atrocious. Your dad suffers from severe dementia, not to mention incontinence (both kinds) and night terrors. And your mother lives in complete denial of reality.

You had to have seen that she was incapable of taking care of that house, or your father, and yet, you put me there to do it. Did you really think that leaving me there was a safe and viable solution?

What was going through your head when you got on that plane, putting three thousand miles between yourself and this ridiculous situation you created?
I didn't even have an address in New York for you.
I guess it was the whole "out of sight, out of mind" thing, but these were your parents, Stephen, not an item of clothing you forgot in a hotel room.
I need you to know, I did the best I could.
I tried to give your parents the love and care that they needed.
Your mom is such a beautiful and gentle spirit, and your dad was clearly so smart. But they can't live in that house anymore without full-time, professional care.
I believe that you knew that. You just didn't want to deal with it.
Hopefully, your sister was able to find the appropriate solutions to care for them.
Almost anything she does will be better than what you did.
Not only did you put your parents' lives at risk, but you also took blatant advantage of me.
That day we met in the juice bar, you saw a vulnerable, scared, desperate young woman, and you found a way to capitalize on that.
I would question whether you were even a doctor, but I know that doesn't have anything to do with it. You can still be a doctor. But you suck as a person, and you are shit for a son.
Rachel

HINDSIGHT

I hate this story. Reading it back, I feel so naive and foolish. I want to reach through the pages and shake that younger version of me. Try to talk some sense into her.

And then I think about just how young I really was. I hadn't ever really been out on my own, and because of that, I had that youthful belief that everyone was inherently good, that people I met would always have my best interest at heart.

In this hindsight, I try to cut myself some slack. I try to see just how fundamentally brave I was—to traverse the country on my own, to be so completely independent. It may have been a mistake, but looking back on it now, it is also damn impressive.

For me, so much of this journey of learning how to speak the fuck up is about examining not only who I am, but who I have been. At twenty-one years old, I was fearless.

When I read this story, I cringe at the fact that I said yes to this clearly terrible idea from a man I had just met. But now, I am *also* going to celebrate my sheer resilience through that situation.

I was broke, and I needed a place to live. I found a solution. It wasn't a good or entirely safe solution for me, but I did my very best. I tried to help two people that needed me, and I got through it.

I am starting to see this chapter in my life through a different lens. I am going to stop being so critical of myself and start recognizing just how strong I have *always* been. Even when I've been scared, and even when I've been compromised, there is a strength inside of me that I can call on.

ONWARDS

Think of a time you've been resilient and strong.

As women, we are so hard on ourselves. It is easy for most of us to think of times we didn't do our best, or when we let someone down. But I guarantee there is a time you can think of when that wasn't the case. There is a time when you did what needed to be done, you handled a situation, you found a way. You were resilient and strong.

Think of this time. Write it down and remind yourself of it. When I first wrote this story, all I saw were my failings. But I now see my strengths. It is essential that we start to celebrate our ability to get to the other side of something, often by sheer will alone.

I promise that if you think of a time you have done this, you will uncover a reservoir of strength within you. You need to be reminded it's there and that you can use it. Write it down and remind yourself of it. It will come in handy later.

Make a list of things you are "grace for."

That is not a typo. We've all heard about the action of making a list of things you are "grateful for" to remind yourself of what really matters, and how much we all already have.

I want you to make a list of things you are *grace* for. Things that challenge you, upset you, compromise you, that you apply your grace to, whether these things deserve it or not.

As I realized in writing this last story, we are often quick to chide ourselves for decisions we make or actions we take. We do this instead of recognizing how much resilience and strength we showed in a situation, just by showing up.

Make a list of times you are "grace for", when you continue to show up despite your decision-making being a little off because you are trying to care for someone or put others first. "Grace for" when the circumstance is unfair, but you must persevere—for money, for family, for survival. Or simply because it is the right thing to do.

Times when you still show up and do the best you can despite how much is stacked against you.

Make that list and then give *yourself* that grace. You are doing what you must do. And you are doing the best you can. Make the list to acknowledge all the hard things you have grace for, and then give yourself that grace.

Ask questions.

As women, we are often so concerned with appearing easygoing and amenable that we fail to ask questions.

When a new opportunity presents itself, we are typically so grateful for the chance that we fail to do our due diligence. We worry that if we ask too many questions, the person extending the opportunity might deem us "difficult" and move on.

I put myself in an insane, "hard to even wrap my head around how I got there" situation at twenty-one years old because I didn't ask any questions.

The right opportunities will not disappear with scrutiny. If they do, they weren't right to begin with.

LANDING IN HOLLYWOOD—#BEFORE #METOO

It took me two days of nonstop driving to get to my uncle's house in Grand Prairie, a suburb about twenty-five minutes outside of Dallas. When I arrived, I was wild-eyed with exhaustion.

Against my better judgment, but fueled by the reality of my finances, I hadn't stopped for the night. I would pull over at rest stops when it was light out, and nap in fifteen minutes increments.

My mom flew in the day before I arrived. When I pulled in, she met me in the driveway. Neither of us had been there before, so we surveyed the place.

It was a huge one-story home that wrapped around an amoeba-shaped swimming pool. The pool was empty save for what looked like five years' worth of leaves and six inches of brown, rancid water.

The rest of the house was not much better. Despite its massive size and high design, my uncle had done nothing to make it a home. The definition of a bachelor, he had one giant leather couch in the living room and an even more egregiously large flat-screen television. In the kitchen, some bar stools were set up around the island. There were piles of unpacked boxes stacked in the hallways. My mom had set up the guest rooms for us. They each contained nothing more than a bed, and in my room, a poster of the Dallas Cowboys Cheerleaders on the wall.

My uncle was nowhere to be found. He spent most of his days at the hospital and went out every night after his rounds. Sometimes he would get home at five a.m., change, and head in to work.

Mom and I spent most of our first days lying on the bare, broken lounge chairs. We had set them up at the edge of the pool and pretended we were on vacation somewhere exotic. Having nothing to do gave us the opportunity to catch up on the last decade of our lives. I had seen my mom during my time at boarding school and college, but this was the longest uninterrupted stretch of time we had spent together. And now, as wounded adults, we were both healing from traumatic experiences. I told her all about living with the old people in Los Angeles. Mom told me about her disastrous second marriage to an environmental lawyer who turned out to be hugely into S&M. She told me that she tried to learn how to be a dominatrix, but instead learned that the roles of S&M don't work that way. We were able to laugh about all of it.

Years later, we would look back on this month and call it "our enchanted April."

One day, we decided to go exploring. I didn't have the money to fill my car with gas, so we set out on a walk. The only option we had was to walk along the highway. We pressed up along the fence and walked three miles until we spotted a strip mall. One of the stores was a Barnes & Noble. We spent the next four hours sitting in leather chairs, in air-conditioning, reading magazine articles to one another.

This experience became a ritual we would repeat many times over the month.

For dinner each night, we would scrounge through my uncle's pantry. We never saw him go shopping, but we kept thinking maybe something new would magically appear. Instead, all we ever found were lots of unopened condiments and a giant barrel of party pretzels. In the freezer was a bucket of premixed margaritas.

Whenever my uncle came home between the hospital and going out for the night, he would walk into the same scene. My mother and I, sitting on top of the kitchen island, the barrel of pretzels between us. We each had spoons in our hands, and we were passing the margarita pail back and forth.

The funny thing is, I remember this as a happy time. I felt like I was getting to know my mother, as an adult, for the first time. I was able to hear her stories about all the hundreds of men she had dated when I was growing up, and not make it about the affect it had on me. I was just happy to be with her. I had felt so lost in Iowa, and so scared in Los Angeles. Being with my mother made me feel like everything was going to be okay. It really was an enchanted April.

The same couldn't be said for the way my uncle was feeling.

One night in early May, my uncle came barging into the house after work and found us having our usual dinner of pretzels and margaritas. He exclaimed, loudly, that he had "had enough!" He said he had made reservations at one of the hot new restaurants in Dallas, and we were to be ready in an hour. A limousine was on its way to take us there.

My mother, not having fully left her "hundreds of men" days behind, got excited. She jumped off the kitchen island to go get ready.

Not me. I held my ground. I told my uncle I would *not* be joining.

My uncle, who I had to admit had *some* say in things, considering he housed and fed us for over a month, looked back at me and said, "Yes. You are." Recognizing this was a battle I was not going to win, I conceded.

"Fine," I answered. And then added, "but I'm not changing!"

I was wearing a pair of ripped jeans and a white T-shirt with a bit of margarita dribble on the front.

An hour later, the limousine pulled into the driveway. Terry, a friend of my uncle's, had already been picked up and was drinking a scotch in the back. We loaded into the limousine. My uncle had on a freshly pressed shirt, and my mom was all done up. I was still in my jeans and T-shirt, with no makeup on and my hair pulled back into a ponytail.

Terry poured a round of champagne and asked if anyone wanted some speed.

"I do!" my mom answered.

I was disgusted. I didn't have any experience with drugs and didn't want to start now. Because I grew up watching both of my parents partake, I was quite a prude, even when it came to drinking. But I was cranky, and now, I was also pissed at my mother. I felt betrayed, alone, and terrified. Instead of acknowledging any of this, I said "fine," and stuck out my hand for the little white pill.

Fifteen minutes later I felt awful. My heart was racing, and I was dripping sweat. When we entered the massive restaurant, I felt like everything was swirling around me. I hated the feeling of being on drugs. I also hated Terry, my uncle, and even my mom in that moment. Everyone else seemed to be having a wonderful time.

While we were waiting for the hostess to seat us, my uncle saw someone he knew and left to say hello. I watched him approach the table of four and shake a man's hand. My mom was watching too and started elbowing me in the ribs. "Isn't that, you know, that director guy you like so much?" she asked.

My crankiness level shot through the roof. I felt like I was living my worst nightmare. One I didn't even know I had. My uncle *was* making small talk with a very famous film director that I immediately recognized. A few years ago, my uncle had been one of the doctors that delivered his son. The director probably had no idea who my uncle was, but he appeared to be acting polite. When my uncle returned to us and we were brought to our table, he was beaming.

I was more than cranky. I was upset. For one of my final projects at Iowa, I had written a paper that questioned whether a male director could tell a women's story. I had focused my hypothesis on this very director. In the paper, I had expressed incredulity at the idea but ended by admitting he had done a good job. I got an A on the paper. That didn't mean I needed to ever meet this director in person. Especially not this night. I had cast myself in the role of "cranky, petulant twenty-one-year-old" for the evening, and I wasn't going to stop now.

We were finishing our appetizers when I felt someone sit down beside me at our banquet. I looked over and it was the Director. The next thing I knew, he was holding my hand and rubbing my forearm. He said, "You have the softest skin I've ever felt." I withdrew my arm and looked at him in silent shock. He went on to motion to my mother sitting next to me. "And the two of you are such a beautiful couple. How long have you been together?"

I recognize this all sounds ridiculous, and it was. I was aware of this in the moment. But every bit of it, however surreal, is true.

I pulled further away from the director and said, as if he were someone I knew and didn't particularly like, "Don't be ridiculous! That's my mother. But I'm gay."

The Director must have found this interesting because he laughed. He stretched out his arms and seemed to be settling in to join us for a while.

In the same annoyed tone I had just used, I pointed to his table and said, "Aren't you on a date?"

The Director glanced over at the three people he had just left, made some grumbling sounds, and went back to his table.

While we were waiting for our entrées, I excused myself and went to the bathroom.

When I came out of the ladies' room, the Director was standing there. He was sort of shuffle-hopping back and forth from one leg to the other. I looked at him. "Do you need to use the restroom?" I asked.

"No, no," he said. "I think we should get out of here. I've called my driver and he's pulling around now. We can sneak out through the back door."

"What?" I asked, feeling entirely sober at this point.

"Yeah, let's get out of here. I want to go somewhere else. I want to go dancing. You must know where we can go dancing?"

The Director wasn't wrong. I had done my "gay research" and found the one strip in Dallas that was gay and full of clubs. I had been to a small lesbian bar called Sue Ellen's but had also taken note of the boys' dance club at the end of the block.

"I only know gay clubs," I said.

"Great!" the Director said. "Let's go!"

We left out the back door. I didn't even go back to the table to say goodbye.

The entire night had been so strange and awful, I figured I had nothing to lose. I was disgusted by the fact that Terry had offered us speed, and disgusted that I had taken it. I hated the way I felt. There was something about the Director that felt a little serendipitous. There was my favorite word again.

Still, it wasn't so much about wanting to be with the Director as it was about not wanting to be where I was. He was offering me a way out.

The moment we got into the car, it felt like the right decision.

I would later find out that the Director was also a Virgo. On that first night, it felt as though we viewed the world through a similar lens. Since I had told him I was gay when he first sat down and made the ridiculous comment about my mother and me, it was as if a line in the sand had been drawn. I had spoken so matter-of-factly about my sexuality, there was no room for him to make an advance. Moreover, were on our way to a gay bar. The energy between us felt electric and conspiratorial, but not sexual.

There was a quality to the Director that was reminiscent of a professor. On the way to the section of the city where the gay clubs are, he had his driver take us on a detour so he could show me where he had filmed his last movie. It was a film about an infamous moment in history. The Director took his time explaining the story to me. He was eager to share a full picture of the event with me, even though he had lived it for years, making the movie. He was giving me the "director's cut" of his blockbuster film. I realized he had a generosity of spirit I had rarely encountered in other people. This, I thought to myself, is truly special, something I will always remember.

When we got to the strip, we started with a drink at Sue Ellen's. This turned into shots with all the women at the bar. We both tried to flirt, but only I was successful. We made our way to the dance club, where the Director continued to buy drinks for anyone in our vicinity. He continued to flirt, this time with shirtless men. It felt harmless and fun, and the boys were loving it. We danced for hours, the Director "whoop, whooping" on the dance floor until they closed the club.

Out of places to go out, we went back to the Mansion at Turtle Creek, where the Director had the penthouse suite. We ordered room service, and the Director made me watch his favorite film, *The Treasure of the Sierra Madre*. He narrated through all of it, pointing out things that made it such a groundbreaking film for its time.

After the film, the Director told me about a new project he was working on. A film about a famous politician. He showed me archival footage of the politician giving speeches. He would point out certain facial expressions and gestures. The Director said these expressions showed the politician was lying. I was bleary eyed, trying to pay attention.

I looked at the clock on the hotel nightstand. It was 5:15 a.m. I told the Director that I had to get back to Grand Prairie because my mother must be worried about me.

The Director jumped up to get his wallet. He handed me a hundred dollars for a taxi back to my uncle's house. I almost didn't take it. I hated the visual of a man handing me money in a hotel room. Even though the evening had been entirely platonic, this simple gesture made it feel dirty. I told the Director as much. Now it was his turn to speak to me matter-of-factly.

"Don't be ridiculous. You have to get home. Take the money."

What I didn't realize at the time was how much of a premonition this moment would turn out to be. In all the years we would spend together, there would always be a difference between the way things looked and the way things were.

I took the money and thanked the Director for an interesting evening.

As I was gathering my things to leave, the Director again spoke to me in the same flat, matter-of-fact tone.

"I've decided. You need to be back in Los Angeles."

I had told the Director about my horrible luck trying to live in Los Angeles. I told him about the Brentwood guesthouse that turned out to be a closet off the laundry room. I shared how I had failed to make any real friends or find any place in L.A. that felt right for me.

The Director told me that Los Angeles "could be the greatest playground in the world" but that I "needed to know where the swing sets were." He said that Los Angeles was a horrible place if you didn't know what you were doing, and a wonderful place if you did.

Right before I walked out the door, he said. "A woman named Annie, from my office, is going to call you tomorrow. You are going to come work for me."

I didn't say anything. The sun was coming up and the night before was already beginning to feel like something in a dream. I left the Mansion on Turtle Creek and took a forty-seven-dollar cab ride home to my uncle's. I remember being delighted that I had so much change from the hundred-dollar bill. My mom and I would both be able to get any magazine we wanted at Barnes & Noble.

The next morning, my mom and I were drinking instant coffee by the pool. We were deciding whether to do our usual walk to Barnes and Noble or try something different. The house phone rang. I went inside to answer.

On the other end of the phone, a woman introduced herself. She explained, rather curtly, that she had "been asked to arrange your transportation back to Los Angeles." I was to arrive on set at the Ritz-Carlton in Pasadena, no later than 8:00 a.m. on Monday.

"Any questions?"

The tone in her voice told me there better not be any questions. She seemed less than happy to be making the call.

On Monday morning, I arrived on the first movie set I had ever set foot on.

A guy wearing a headset, with a walkie-talkie attached to his belt buckle, led me over to the Director. He was sitting in a chair, watching a monitor in front of him. On the screen was a famous male actor, done up to look just like the politician.

"Ah good, you're here," the Director said.

I was. And I would stay by his side for the next four years.

Not one day of those four years was easy. What I had failed to account for when I said yes to the job was what it would look like to other people. It was the curse of the hundred-dollar bill in the hotel room. What people thought and what the truth was . . . were very different things.

From the moment I walked onto the set in Pasadena, everyone thought I was sleeping with the Director. I can't really blame them. Filming had already started, and I just appeared out of nowhere. On the call sheet, I was listed as the Director's personal assistant.

No one on set even tried to make it a secret what they thought of me.

It felt like all anyone would talk about. There was almost constant murmuring every time I walked into a room. It didn't help that I was the only assistant assigned to the Director. He would ask me to attend the lunches and dinners in his trailer, along with the film's star and the director of photography. To everyone else, it looked like I was being given preferential treatment.

In reality, the Director never personally acknowledged me on set. He would ask that I take notes in every meeting. He would yell at me if I didn't record things perfectly.

I felt completely isolated and alone on that set. For four months, I didn't talk to anyone all day except the Director. The other production assistants were always sitting together, eating together. The days I wasn't in a lunch with the Director, I would eat alone, crouched behind the craft service truck.

This loneliness was nothing compared to the way the other men on the set treated me. Specifically, the men in power-The actors, the producers, the writers.

These men must have also thought I was sleeping with the Director, because they all treated me like I was something they could acquire. They took huge liberties with their words and actions. Every day after lunch, I would knock on the trailer door of one of the lead actors. My job was to tell him it was time to come back from break. Every day, he would open the door totally naked. He would hold his dick in his hand, gently rubbing it, and ask me if I wanted to come inside.

The producers were even worse. When we finished filming and went into postproduction, I had to share an office with two of them. Technically, they had the offices, and I had a desk outside. I was groped, squeezed, pinched, or fondled every time they walked by my desk. They were constantly making comments about my weight, my hair, my outfits. One of them would leave his office door open while he described, in great detail, his sexual conquests of the night before.

Everything came to a head the night of the wrap party. I had never been to a wrap party before and had no idea what to expect. I also had no idea what to wear. I settled on a spaghetti-strap black dress. I didn't own any other shoes besides sneakers or flip-flops, so I wore my black Teva sandals.

An hour into the party, the Director called me over to where he was sitting. He was at a large round table in the corner of the room, surrounded by eight other men, mostly actors from the film. The Director informed me I would be going to Washington, DC, with him in the morning. He was going to shoot some second unit footage for the film.

After he told me this, he looked me up and down for a long moment. And then he declared, in front of everyone, "You can wear that dress again, but change your fucking shoes."

Of all the things that had ever been said to me, or about me, *this* was the thing that shook me up. I backed away from the table, unable to form a response.

All I could think was "Why does what I'm wearing matter to the shooting of this film?" It was a rhetorical question. I already had my answer.

What I was wearing was the only thing that mattered.

I wasn't there on set every day because of my talents or skills. I was there because of the way I looked. It was a truth I had known from the very beginning but had chosen to ignore.

Something about the setting, the way men were sitting around the Director, leering at me, and laughing when he said it, that pushed me over the edge.

In that moment, all the rage I had suppressed, all the times I had been rendered speechless by the shocking bad behavior of so many of the men I had met on film sets and in the production office, came flooding through me.

I left the party and quit the next day. I never went to Washington.

Instead, I wrote the Director a letter and had it dropped off at his house before he left for the airport.

I spoke the fuck up.

To my surprise, the Director apologized and asked if I would come back and work in a research capacity on his next film. I did go back for a short while, but things didn't feel the same. It was like I had lost some of my shine, in his eyes. I do believe he tried to do the right thing by me, but he ultimately didn't know what that was.

For years, I had a front-row seat to observe the power dynamic that exists in Hollywood. This powerful male Director had carte blanche when it came to his behavior. Especially with women. There were so many times I would arrange a lunch meeting for an aspiring actress or send one of them back to his office for a meeting, and the door would always be closed. I had no idea what was being talked about or what was being said or done.

The #MeToo movement would later expose a lot of the disgusting behavior of men in Hollywood. It would shed light on the abuse and assaults that were commonplace in the entertainment industry. It would reveal the incredibly deep-seated misogyny.

But only a little bit.

The degradation and commodification of women is the most defining quality of Hollywood. It was everywhere, and it was inescapable.

I have wondered if I was complicit because I didn't speak the fuck up every time I saw something that could potentially put a woman in a vulnerable position.

I know that I was put there, over and over again.

I did write one letter. But it wasn't enough. It barely scratched the surface.

Dear Director,

I am sure this will not come as any surprise to you, but I am quitting again.

This time, I won't come back. I don't want to be within one hundred miles of the world you created. A world that treats women as less than. A world that hurts them.

When we met, I was so young. I instinctively knew to protect myself, my sexuality, from you. I put up a barrier that you knew not to cross, but still, you compromised me in every way. Not as a gay woman. As a woman, period. Even though you never touched me and never made an advance on me, I felt completely compromised. You created a culture of misogyny, and every woman around you was in danger. It was a shark tank, and women were chum. I felt completely exposed and unprotected.

You were totally removed. You never had to face any assumptions or opinions about yourself. The leering looks, the sense of feeling like property, never affected you. It was your world.

You were king.

All around you there was disgusting behavior by men towards me, and you never once did anything to correct any of them. Why would you? My being there added to your power. I was your conquest. Even though I wasn't. You showed me a world almost anyone would have been thrilled to see. I know I had a job ten thousand film-school students would have killed for.

But it wasn't worth it. Not one day of it was worth it. Working for you has completely traumatized me. It was a slow and insidious process, but somehow, you stripped me of all my sense of self. You made me doubt I could advocate for myself, protect myself, or be seen for anything more than my physical appearance. You made me doubt I had anything more to offer.
When I think about the actresses you cast in your films, I want to throw up.
Did things happen to them because you single-handedly had the ability to make or break their careers? Their entire futures, financially and career-wise, in that moment of decision, were up to you.
What price did you make them pay for your "Yes"?
It all makes sense now. Why you had to surround yourself with such vile, disgusting men. They made you look better. But not really. Not to anyone paying attention.
The fact that you didn't have even one woman in any position of power around you makes perfect sense. If they had risen to that stature in Hollywood, they would have called you out on your bullshit.
I may still be powerless in that town, but now I am calling you on your bullshit.
No career advancement, no opportunity, no proximity to the most glamorous of all worlds, Hollywood, is worth being put in such a threatening and dangerous position every single day.
In the end, instead of giving me an opportunity to have a career in moviemaking, something I would have loved to do, you made me never, ever want to work in that town again.
I am not safe.
And you are not benevolent.
From my vantage point, no amount of brilliance can hide a misogynist and a predator or cleanse a tarnished soul.
Rachel

Dear Producer,

(Ten Years Later)
We just got off the phone a little while ago.
It was shocking to hear from you so many years later.
I'm glad you got yourself help, and that you are working the program.
I guess this means that I was one of your steps.
Did you have to make three hundred calls? Three thousand?
It's all true, and you are correct. You were atrocious.
Every single day that I was in that office with you felt like a fight to protect myself and my body from you.
If it wasn't your creepy shoulder rubs and squeezes, it was your lascivious looks, your prying into my dating life, and the disgusting accounts of your dating life.
I had to spend eight hours a day, every day, at my desk outside your office, looking at you with your feet up on your desk, leaning back in your leather chair, shouting things at me.
You could never just ask me something without some reference to a body part or a sexual act.
I can still hear you shout from your desk, "Bring that ass in here!"
When you were walking by my desk, if you didn't touch me, you inevitably made a comment about how my tits looked in whatever shirt I was wearing. "Fantastic" or "Not enough!" You would always let me know.
When your comments or advances were not directed at me, I felt even more disgusted. It was even harder for me to hear the way you talked about other women. In fact, in all the hundreds of audition assessments I heard you give, I never once heard you talk about an actress's acting ability. Her fuckability, yes. Who she had already fucked, yes. Her acting, not once.
After every audition, I was privy to a lengthy breakdown

of her entire body, how much you did or didn't want to fuck her, and when you would.
I believe women meant nothing to you. You had a wife and daughter. They could not have meant anything to you, the way you behaved.
I was a young woman who was completely dependent on my weekly paycheck to live.
You were a wealthy man with all the power in the world to control my financial security and that of dozens of other women.
You made the choice, every single day, to be a predatory asshole.
You were an overweight, balding monster who had cigar-stained teeth and reeked of body odor. And you preyed on women.
I am glad you got sober, but I think there is a bigger fish to fry here.
Are you using your addiction to excuse your behavior all those years?
No offense to AA, but that sucks eggs. And it's not enough.
I can hear your apology. I appreciate it, but I don't accept it.
I took your call, but don't think that in my mind you are absolved for what you did, or that your actions didn't have a lasting impact.
Because they did.
Rachel

HINDSIGHT

When the #MeToo movement exploded into the cultural zeitgeist, every memory I had about my time in Hollywood came rushing back to me. I heard my own story in so many of the stories that were just then coming out.

When I was working in Hollywood, it was such a different time. Nobody, and I mean nobody, spoke up.

My hindsight from this experience is just how pervasive the culture of misogyny was, and how hard it was to see what was happening all around me. It was so "normal" for women to be seen as objects and commodities that it felt almost impossible to speak up about blatant abuse.

I now understand just how truly dangerous this is. When a culture, like the one that existed in Hollywood when I was working there, becomes so entwined with the fabric of the industry, it's impossible to separate the two.

I know it may be hard to imagine, but it truly was *everywhere.* I think about the excuse some people make to justify their bad behavior: "That's just the way it was back then." Hollywood in the 1990s felt like this justification on steroids.

Add to this the wild economic disparity that existed between the men in power and the women that worked for them, and you have the perfect recipe for abuse and misogyny. The men that were verbally and physically violating me were also paying me. I was dependent on them for my livelihood. I try to believe that if, back then, I had the self-worth and the voice that I do now, I would have spoken up. But I was twenty-four years old, living three thousand miles away from home, paycheck to paycheck, completely alone.

I had landed in one of the most extreme cultures against women that there was.

Mostly, my hindsight is that I am glad it is behind me, and I am grateful there are women speaking the fuck up about it now.

ONWARDS

Examine your work environment.

What I learned from my experience in Hollywood is that your environment is everything. The environment of a workplace creates the culture of that workplace. And that culture will dictate how you are treated and how you will feel being there.

Whether you have been someplace for ten years or are just thinking about taking a new job, spend a bit of time examining the environment.

Are women in positions of power? Do you feel like they are respected in the way men speak in the office, either about female colleagues or women in general? Have you witnessed or heard something that could be harmful to a woman, or yourself, only to get the sense that everyone else is desensitized? That that type of behavior is "just the way it is"?

If any of these things ring true, recognize that you are not in a culture that is safe, and that your work environment may slowly be eroding your self-esteem and sense of worth.

Hollywood is an extreme example, but not an isolated one. For this Onwards, ask yourself if you really feel safe in the place(s) where you spend your days.

Dear Reader,

I wanted to take a moment to check in.

At this point in my stories, I am in my early twenties, and everything feels a bit unmoored.

I imagine reading about it feels the same.

In these stories, I feel messy and lost because I was.

Yet the version of me in my twenties is also one of my favorites. She is probably the one I would choose to take to a desert island.

I had different kinds of survival skills back then. I had zero skills for becoming successful or creating a sustainable life for myself. But I did seem to have the ability to get myself into wild situations, and to always get myself out. I always seemed to land on my feet.

I mention this to you as I am aware the twenties version of me may not seem the most reliable narrator.

But she is getting there. She is discovering herself and shaping herself, and she has a kind of strength and survival instinct that is worth illuminating.

In these stories, I can also begin to see the things in me that kept me from speaking the fuck up.

The situations and cultures I put myself in, coupled with my insistence on "going it alone" and not needing anyone, often put me in compromised positions.

I believe we gravitate toward situations that are comfortable and familiar, even if they aren't good for us.

Some of the dynamics I experienced in my twenties, most notably in Hollywood, serve as a blueprint for later situations. They were situations I could recognize. So, I went toward them.

The work of tracing back threads that start in your adolescence and young adulthood will be revelatory to your understanding of why and where you are on your own journey of speaking the fuck up.

My guess is that you will have the same revelation I am having.

Something is always the same.

There is always one common thread.

That's the thing that must be revealed to shove us into speaking the fuck up. It starts with finding that thing.

And now, at the insistence of my favorite word:

Onwards!

Yours,

Rachel

A "BIG FISH" INDEED

When I quit my job in the movie industry, I had to figure out a way to pay rent. Working for the Director was the first time in my life I had a steady paycheck, and now that had ended. I also needed to find a new place to live. When we were on location, I lived in long-stay hotels or in arranged housing. The last two years of working for the Director, I had lived in his guesthouse. (At least I had made that tiny dream come true.)

Since moving to Los Angeles, I had only ever explored the West Side, because I was so enchanted by the Pacific Ocean. I found a small apartment in Santa Monica. The apartment itself was nothing special, but it was a straight shot, twenty-six blocks, to the beach. I settled into my new home and started thinking about what jobs I could do.

There was a very small window of time after I left working for the Director that I tried to be an actor. This was not something I sought out. I had gone alone to the concert of a female indie-rock singer that I liked. A woman approached me at the concert and asked me if I had ever considered acting. I told her I hadn't. She handed me her business card and told me to call her office.

It felt like one of those "nothing to lose" moments. After taking a meeting at her office and reading some sides (a part of a scene from a movie or show) for her, I proved, without a doubt, that I could not act.

She told me she wanted to enroll me in an intensive acting class. She said that I had a "look" that everyone wanted right now.

I was newly unemployed, without any idea of my next step. I took the classes, and she sent me on about four auditions a day over the next three months.

I didn't get a single job. "She can't act her way out of a paper bag" was the feedback every casting director would send back to my agent. They would all mention how personable I was, how great I was at chitchat before the audition. But they would always end by telling my agent some version of "I would rather cut my eyes out than have to watch her try to act again."

The one good thing that came out of all this was that my agent suggested I get a job to support my going on auditions. She told me to do what thousands of other aspiring actors in Los Angeles do: get a job waiting tables. It would keep my days free to audition.

I tried to imagine this. I had bused tables when I was in high school, but I had never served anyone food. I could be quite a picky eater. I imagined having to deal with other people's weird eating issues. It didn't feel like the right move for me.

On a bike ride to the beach one morning, I passed a large hotel on the corner of Ocean Avenue and Pico Boulevard, called Shutters on the Beach. Something about the building itself made me stop. Shutters stood out from the other hotels along the strip of beach in Santa Monica. It was white and crisp looking, more classic than Californian. When I picked up a brochure, the marketing touted how it was designed to "feel like Cape Cod."

I felt a sense of nostalgia. The design did remind me of where I was from. I liked the juxtaposition of Shutters and the Pacific Ocean, which was fifty yards from the hotel steps.

I decided to ask if they were hiring for any positions. I was informed they were currently hiring for the lobby lounge. Specifically, the man at the front desk told me they were hiring "lobby lounge girls."

I took a seat and filled out the application. I lied and listed a couple of bars in Iowa that I had worked at. I had been to the bars, once. I figured it couldn't be that hard to work there. I hadn't considered that they might call to check references. They didn't.

I got the job. A few days later, I was in training with five other women hired at the same time. We were to be the new class of Shutters on the Beach lobby lounge girls.

As a lobby lounge girl, my job was to serve the customers, hotel guests, and locals that came to sit in the lobby of the hotel. We took orders from our tables and entered them at one of our two computer stations. To pick up the drinks, we had to walk through the lobby, around the corner, and up the eight steps to the main restaurant. During our mock service, I made my way to the bar, and just as I was about to put my drinks on my tray, the woman behind me whispered, "Other hand."

I was about to carry my tray in my right hand, which would have meant I had to serve with my left hand. I was right-handed. I would have spilled the drinks everywhere.

Picking up those drinks during the training was the first time I had ever carried a tray. That lobby lounge girl saved me.

The Shutters lobby was a beautiful room framed by floor-to-ceiling windows that looked out onto the Pacific. Along the windows, there was a row of two-top tables for couples, some larger four tops in the center of the room and three couch areas for larger groups. In one corner, a grand piano sat by the two tables designated as the smoking section. Tucked in the back of the room was a fireplace and another low-seating couch area.

I loved this room. The most coveted seats were just outside the lobby, on the patio overlooking the boardwalk and the Pacific Ocean. Everyone wanted to sit out there. I loved working outside on the patio. I also loved the section in the back, the smoking couch section. The customers were fascinating. Outside on the patio were the young movie stars, the Chicago ad-agency guys, and the guys trying to impress first dates. On the smoking couches were the agents, the producers, and the rock stars in recovery. They would drink soda water with lime and go through two packs of cigarettes. I got the hang of serving drinks quickly and was one of the most popular lobby lounge girls. I was a hard worker, and reliable. I was never late for a single shift and would pick up other people's shifts last minute. I loved my job.

My favorite part was the short, but intimate, conversations I could have with my tables. Most of the time, I was serving alcohol, which meant my customers were usually in a good mood. They would ask me questions about myself. I would talk about my surfing or my writing.

I was both enigmatic and an open book.

I made great money, going home some nights with $500 in tips.

I look back on those two years at Shutters as some of the best of my life.

It's interesting to me, the judgment we can place on ourselves. Despite being happier and more peaceful than I had ever been, I chastised myself for not doing more.

I didn't consider my waitressing job a "real" career.

I wish I had the hindsight I do now.

That job was a perfect fit for me. I was respected by my customers and colleagues. I was instantly rewarded for my ability to remember things. I could take the drink order for a table of eight without writing anything down. And I always had a positive attitude.

If ever a customer made an off-color comment or behaved disrespectfully, my manager would have them escorted out immediately. It was clear to the manager that I was valuable to their bottom line. Every night, customers would call ahead to request my section.

For one six-month period, I had to come in every Sunday and work brunch, because Ronald Reagan requested that he always be sat in my section. This was wild to me. I was young when he was the president. I hated his politics and his devastating response to the AIDS crisis.

Still, when he came in on Sundays and took my hand, looking up at me with those famous blue eyes, all I saw was an old, fragile man. One that was grateful to see a familiar, smiling face.

I knew he was suffering from dementia, but there was always at least one instance during every brunch when he would recognize me and call me by my name. "Rachel. How are you? How was your week?" Ronald Reagan would ask.

I often wonder how my life would have been different without my internal judgment that I couldn't be "just a waitress." I had this idea that I had to be something "more."

I have so many more lovely stories from this time, one in particular, that I will never forget.

This memory reminds me that speaking the fuck up is not always an angry or defiant act; it can also be wonderful. Sometimes, speaking the fuck up is being able to say the words "I love you" or "Thank you."

In this case, speaking the fuck up is saying, "You really made a difference in my life."

This letter was easy to write. This letter was awesome to write.

This letter is not anonymous.

Dear Albert Finney,

I wish I had sent this letter to you when you were still alive. I am writing it now because I want to celebrate the amazing person you were. And I want other people to know too.

You spent almost a year at Shutters when I was working there. It was the year you were Oscar nominated for your part in Erin Brockovich.

You should have won!

I still giggle to myself when I remember how you invited me to a pre-Oscar cocktail party in your room. You said it was just going to be you, your partner Pene, and Julia.

At least I thought you said Julia, as in Julia Roberts, which made sense because she was in the movie with you. When I got to your room, I met your agent. Julian. Truth be told, that was a bummer.

I saw you and your beautiful wife, Pene, nearly every single day for the entire year, which is quite remarkable when you think about it.

Sometimes it would just be for a quick scotch after you had both been out and about.

More often, it would be when I served your decadent, drawn-out and languorous late-afternoon lunches.

When I saw you two come in, I would find the restaurant manager and tell him I was serving lunch in the lobby. They couldn't say no to me.

I loved when you two would have these lunches with me. You would order a few bottles of wine, lobster salads and dessert. I would serve the full meal to the two of you, as you lounged on the couch by the fireplace. Often, I felt like it was the three of us having lunch together.

You would always offer me wine, even though you knew I couldn't accept.

It didn't matter. I always felt drunk on your company. I loved your smile, your accent, and the way that you and Pene would still kiss like schoolkids.

The two of you would always ask me how my writing was going.

You were the first people I told that I wanted to write a nonfiction book called The Great American Waitress.

I shared my plan to travel across the country interviewing waitresses. I wanted to go to all sorts of restaurants. From the most expensive to the roadside diner. I wanted to write about how waitressing was a profession that afforded women financial independence. I wanted to explore the history and the impact of the profession on the feminist movement.

You and Pene thought this was a great idea.

Still, I was shocked when, after our last long lunch together, on the day the two of you left to return to London, you did something extraordinary. You left me a $10,000 tip.

I can't tell you how much I cried, standing in that lobby.
You had written on the check "For your book."
It was the most special thing anyone had ever done for me.
I haven't finished the book yet. I'm sorry.
I spent every cent of your money renting a van and driving across the country interviewing waitresses. I brought a photographer with me, and she took incredible pictures of the waitresses we found. It was amazing. I wish you could see the interviews. I know this book really could have been something.
I stopped because I ran out of money and needed to get back to California and start working again. I really hope I finish the book someday. It will be dedicated to you.
There is a song I remember from childhood.
It is something about "if just one person believes in you."
I think it's from a Charlie Brown holiday special.
Albert, you were that person for me. And you made me believe in me, too.
From the bottom of my heart.
Thank you.
Yours,
Rachel

HINDSIGHT

I love this story. I need this story. So much of my twenties was wild, weird, odd, and sometimes dangerous. But much of it was serendipitous (the good kind), revelatory, and wonderful. Getting to know Albert Finney was wonderful.

A lot of the stories in this book are about men that didn't know how to use their power for good, or who couldn't escape their own egos and insecurities to trust and respect women.

My hindsight from this story is that there are good men—there are great men—out there. They have power, and they don't use it to exploit, abuse, undermine, or silence women.

I have met many of them, and I take joy in knowing they exist. I have never been the type of woman, or specifically, the type of gay woman, to dislike men. I don't think many of us are. The stereotype that society has placed on us, suggesting that we dislike men, simply isn't true.

I like anyone that knows how to treat people with decency, respect, and basic humanity.

And yes, sometimes these people happen to be men.

P.S.—The title of this chapter comes from a great Albert Finney film, *Big Fish*. If you haven't seen it, go watch it.

ONWARDS

Ask yourself "Who do you love?"*

*(And do they know it?)

I have the Bo Diddley song in my head as I write this. It's a great song and an even better question.

For this Onwards, ask yourself this question, and make a list of the answers. There will be the obvious ones, and then, probably, some people that surprise you. Think about those people.

Do they know that you love them?

Maybe. But maybe not. Or maybe they could use a reminder.

That is what this Onwards is about—sending that reminder. It can be a text or a call or a good old-fashioned letter in the mail. Use your voice and tell someone that you love them, or that you appreciate them and respect them.

It may literally take ten seconds, but I guarantee that you (and they) will feel an incredible, lasting effect from saying something. It is so simple and yet so powerful to just say, "Hey, I'm thinking about you, and I love you. I am so grateful you are in my life."

THE DEVIL WEARS TWEED

There would never be another customer like Albert Finney. He was one of a kind. When Albert and Pene returned to London, my afternoon shifts got a lot less fun.

I had some favorite regulars who would come at night, but the hours between two and seven p.m. would often drag for me.

It didn't help that there was much less drinking happening in the afternoon. During these hours my customers tended to be businesspeople in town for meetings. I had many solo coffee drinkers. And anyone that has worked in a restaurant knows that there is no downer quite like multiple cappuccino orders.

One afternoon, a much older man approached the service station and asked me if he could get a sandwich in the lobby. I rarely asked to make this exception unless it was for Albert and Pene. But there was not another customer in the entire lobby. At least I would have something to do for twenty minutes while this man ate his lunch.

After he had finished his sandwich, he tried to strike up a conversation with me. There was something about him that immediately put me off. His eyeglasses were badly smudged, and he was wearing one of those tweed blazers with leather patches at the elbow. He was tall and thin, but I could see a little belly pushing out of his shirt. He had a musty smell and he appeared to be at least seventy years old. He looked like a writer, and I would soon discover that he was.

I stood a few feet away from him when he started asking me questions about what I did and what other things I was interested in.

I wanted a good tip on the only bill over twenty dollars that I had that day. I told him I wanted to be a writer. I didn't get into the specifics of *The Great American Waitress.* I was trying to end the conversation when the writer told me he was a contributing editor at my favorite magazine.

The magazine was one I had always dreamed of writing for. More than any other publication, I daydreamed about seeing my name in print in its pages. Fiction or nonfiction. It didn't matter to me if it was in this magazine. I loved the cover and the font and the way the titles of the articles floated in the middle of the page. I loved everything about the magazine.

Now, I was curious about this man. "Why are you in Los Angeles?" I asked him.

In an ironic twist of fate, the writer told me he was there to do an interview with the same director I had worked for a few years ago. When I mentioned this to the writer, he found it very interesting.

He went on to tell me that from Los Angeles he was going on to Las Vegas to cover ShoWest, a conference I had heard about but had never attended. The writer explained that ShoWest was the biggest convention in the world for the film business, and every major celebrity would be there. He mentioned that the magazine had assigned him a feature-length article on the conference, and the angle was to follow the owner of the largest theater chain in the country as he made decisions about which films to buy. It was going to be an inside look at the "business of film."

The writer finished his sandwich and returned to the service station. He said that he had an idea: He would have a chat with the Director. If the Director vouched for me, the writer would call his boss at the magazine and request permission to bring me to Las Vegas as a writer's assistant.

I could hardly believe what this man was offering. Writing for this particular magazine would be my *biggest* dream come true. I didn't ask questions. I didn't do my research. I just said yes.

The writer returned a few days later to tell me it was all set up. He said he had spoken to the Director, who had sung my praises. The writer told me I would receive a stipend of $150 a day, for nine days.

The magazine would pay me at the end of our time in Las Vegas.

I couldn't believe I would be getting a paycheck from the magazine I read cover to cover every week.

The writer told me that if I did a good job in Las Vegas, he was confident the magazine would hire me full-time. It all felt so serendipitous. Even though it would require moving back across the country, the magazine was worth it.

I was in.

A week before, while walking to my car after an evening shift, I had been held up at gunpoint, and I was still quite shaken up about it. This felt like the right moment to take a break from Los Angeles. My boss at Shutters was understanding and assured me that I always had had a place there. I knew it was true, but the fact that I was going to be paid to be a writer, for my favorite magazine no less, made my decision to leave Los Angeles easy.

There was a lot I had to pull together to leave for Las Vegas in three days. I subleased my apartment and loaded my Jeep Cherokee with my belongings. I didn't have many things I cared about, so there wasn't too much to pack. My clothes, some paintings, and my bicycle, which I attached to the back of the jeep.

I arrived in Las Vegas and checked in to the New York-New York hotel, which was the cheapest one I could find. The writer said he was checking on getting reimbursement for my travel expenses and was waiting to hear back. I think the room was forty-nine dollars a night, which I could manage.

I had to pay extra to park my car at the hotel, and the parking cost was more than the rate of the room. I had just enough money to cover everything until I received my check. I should have had some savings, but at this time in my life, I was very much living paycheck to paycheck. I had one week of tips saved for this trip. My plan was to drive to New York and stay with my grandmother in Yonkers until I could afford a place in the city, as a writer at the magazine.

The writer was staying at the MGM Grand, where most of the conference was being held. He asked me to come to his hotel room the night before the conference started to make our plan. In his room, he opened a bottle of wine and talked about his past writing achievements. We didn't talk about the upcoming week.

The next morning, we met the theater owner for breakfast. He had flown in from Texas and looked every bit the part. He was wearing boots, jeans, a giant brass-buckled belt, and a cowboy hat. Just what I would expect from a rich Texas businessman. He shook my hand, winked, and told me to call him by his first name.

The breakfast went well. I had tucked myself into the corner to take notes, but the theater owner insisted I sit at the table along with the writer. During this first interview, the theater owner was relaxed and friendly. He would often refer to me directly, asking me questions about what I liked in movies.

The theater owner invited me to sit next to him when the three of us went to one of the first big events of the conference. It was a lunch during which the stars of that year's upcoming films would introduce the films they were in. "Have you ever seen a movie star beg?" the theater owner leaned over and asked me.

"Get ready."

I realized that in this situation, the theater owner had all the power. He was making decisions on whether to buy a particular film or not.

The writer seemed annoyed by the attention I was receiving from the theater owner. The writer grew increasingly curt with me. He would snap at me if I tried to engage in conversation. I had barely said anything to the theater owner except to answer his direct questions.

Every night after dinner, I would go to the writer's hotel room to review the day's notes.

On the fifth night in Las Vegas, I returned to my hotel before heading to the writer's room. In my room, on the pillow, was a box and a note.

I opened the box. It was a one-inch-thick diamond bracelet. The note was from the theater owner, thanking me for making his days "a lot shinier." In the note, he invited me to come to Texas to visit him after the conference.

I was shocked and speechless. I packed up the bracelet and the note and went to the writer's hotel room. I thought he could help me make sense of it and that together, we could figure out what to do.

When I showed the writer the note, his entire face turned purple. He screamed that "he knew it" and pushed me against the door of the hotel room. He continued screaming, inches from my face. He accused me of sleeping with the theater owner. He shouted that he had brought me here, insisting that I "belonged to him." He put his hands under my shirt on my breasts and neck.

In a state of panic, I swung my arms and hit the writer in the face with my laptop. He stumbled backward and then lunged at me. I pushed him to the ground and ran out of the room.

He was screaming at me as I ran down the hallway.

When I got back to my hotel, I was crying hysterically. The writer left a message on the hotel room phone that I was a "filthy whore" and telling me that I was dead to him. He said that I would never work at my favorite magazine, or at any magazine for that matter. He told me I was a fool if I thought there was any other reason for my being there other than because I looked like I "would be good in bed."

I never got paid by the magazine. I have no idea if anyone at the magazine even knew about me.

I never heard from the writer again.

The article did come out. It was a less-than-glowing portrait of the theater owner.

Dear writer,

You disgust me.
I feel like I have almost nothing to say to you, but I will think of a few things.
I should have recognized your smarminess the first time we met.
The lenses of your glasses were all smudged. Your teeth were yellow. Your breath smelled like you had eaten a decaying rat.
You were the rat.
You thought that using four-syllable words would impress me.
I should have seen you coming a mile away.
When you started talking to me, I was just being polite. And it wasn't easy.
When you said you worked for my favorite magazine, I let something in my mind recast you.
I stopped seeing you as a pathetic, lecherous pig. Instead, I reframed you as an intellectual.
That's on me. But the rest of it, every bit of it, is on you. You violated me, and you assaulted me.
From what I experienced, I am positive I am not the only woman you hurt.
You are a sad and pathetic excuse for a man, and all your "literary accomplishments" don't cover up the truth of who you are.
I got away from you, but you will have to live with yourself forever.
You will have to grow older, and die, knowing that you are a disgraceful piece of shit.
I hope the laptop hurt.
Rachel

HINDSIGHT

This story, maybe more than any other in this book, was a hard one to tell. For so many years, when I looked back on this event, I would think about how I let myself down. I would berate myself for being so trusting and willing to heedlessly believe in someone, with no real evidence or proof that what they were saying was true.

I would get so upset at myself for actively ignoring my instincts for an opportunity I didn't think I could get on my own. I hated that I didn't have the faith in my abilities or intuition to walk away from something that never felt quite right.

Now, I see this story differently. What the writer did was atrocious. He was a predator that assaulted me. He orchestrated a situation that would put me in a place (literally and figuratively) of vulnerability and without protection or a place to run.

This story is one of the starkest examples of how my lack of voice and my inability to speak the fuck up jeopardized my safety. If I had asked questions, done some research, and legitimized what the writer was offering, I wouldn't have put myself in that position. And that is my responsibility. To look out for myself. But at the end of the day, there will always be men that manipulate and take advantage of a woman's trust.

And this is not the woman's fault.

We do not have to change who or how we are.

But we do have to speak the fuck up, always, and loudly when something isn't right.

LATER HINDSIGHT

During the editing process, I took a break from writing this chapter to watch a documentary about a famous actor. The first episode starts out exploring how such a beloved star could suffer such a fall from grace. The next episodes examine his family and its specific legacy of misogyny and abuse. I turned this documentary on because I remember reading the headlines and being curious about what the story was all about. I didn't know anything about the rest of the family and found it fascinating. Halfway through a later episode, there is an interview with a writer who was hired in 1980 by a well-known newspaper to write a profile on one of the family members.

I looked up at my TV screen to see the writer who assaulted me. For the next ten minutes, I listened to him explain how his profile subject created a public persona purposely separate from his private activities, how controlling he was of everyone around him, and how despicable he was to women.

The part that really got me, and the part I cannot unhear, is the writer explaining how his subject specifically looked for young women that he could control completely. It was the writer's assertion that this man saw women as objects and not as human beings.

It will take me a long time to recover from hearing my abuser speak about someone doing exactly what he did to me.

At this point in my journey of learning how to speak the fuck up, I think I must be getting somewhere because watching this documentary, and hearing the writer talk about the same behaviors I saw in him, makes me want to fucking scream.

ONWARDS

Find your intuition and then sit with her.

So obvious and so easy to *say*, but remarkably harder to do. As I wrote this Onwards, my fingers on the keyboard accidentally typed "her" instead of "it." I'm not changing it. Intuition is conscious and conscientious. She is deep, nurturing, aware, and sensory.

Of course she is a woman!

When you hear the female voice of intuition talking to you—listen. Sit still with her, for hours or days if necessary, and keep checking back in with her. Intuition and impulsive decisions are not compatible. She will serve as a checkpoint for you on the road, slowing you down before you do something rash.

Your intuition asks you to take your time, to ask questions, and to consider and then reconsider everything. The next time you find yourself at a crossroads, or facing a tough decision, find your intuition and then sit with her. Much like the other women you encounter on this journey, she will listen, she will be patient, and she will not let you down.

BE DIFFICULT.

Another all-caps Onwards! This one feels so important to say and to hear.

As women, we are taught that we must *not* be difficult. We're discouraged from asking too many questions, expressing concerns, or challenging what's presented to us. This pervasive social conditioning, which most women encounter, is precisely what sustains the dominant paradigm.

It's crucial to understand that asking questions and voicing concerns is *not* being "difficult." It's a display of self-awareness, a means of protecting oneself, and a way of being proactive. It is advocating for yourself, your children, your relationships, and your talents. It's about demanding what you rightfully deserve.

Asking for more information means getting what you need to make an informed decision, one that is in your best interest.

If something is broken and not working, the behavior that society deems as "being difficult" is what gets it fixed.

Women are expected to shrink and "shush" to fit into society's standards of what a pleasing and appealing woman should be. Enough with that bullshit.

Be difficult and be beautiful in doing so.

If it helps, imagine your child or a friend watching you speak up for what you know is right. Don't you want them to see that example? I can assure you they won't perceive you as difficult. Instead, they will see you as capable and empowered. They will see you as a hero.

THE ANGEL WEARS NATORI

I stood in the lobby of the MGM Grand casino reflecting on the events that had led me to that moment. I had left behind a fantastic job and a great apartment in Los Angeles to pursue a dream in New York City. Ten minutes ago, I was fondled and threatened by a disgusting and lecherous man, who then made it abundantly clear that my dream was never going to happen. And then I hit him with my laptop and fled into the lobby.

Now, I was stranded in Las Vegas.

It is a unique and specific thing to feel your entire world crumble while standing in the middle of a Las Vegas casino floor. But there I was. I was also almost thirty years old, homeless, and unemployed.

I made my way back to New York-New York—the hotel, not the city. I now had to foot the hotel bill and the cost of the garage, where my car was stored with all my belongings in the trunk.

I stood in yet another casino lobby, trying to hear my thoughts above the dinging and cha-chinging of the slot machines. I desperately needed air. Instead, I inhaled the smoke and fumes of thin hope and heavily shattered dreams that stand in for oxygen in Las Vegas.

I used the hotel phone to call my grandmother in Yonkers, and I told her what had happened.

The next morning, she wired me enough money to get my car out of the garage and make my way back to the East Coast.

I made it to Yonkers, where I spent two full weeks licking my wounds and feeling sorry for myself. I ate a lot of my grandma's lasagna and watched *Wheel of Fortune* with her every evening.

There is a quote about how it "is always darkest, just before the dawn."

Going from thinking I was going to be a writer at my favorite magazine to engaging in nightly *Wheel of Fortune* viewing was a dark place for me.

It was time to figure out what I could do for work again.

I went through the want ads in the local paper.

One morning, I walked the mile from my grandmother's modest house on Tuckahoe Road to the Central Avenue Deli. I applied for a job slicing meat. The man behind the counter asked me if I had ever worked in a deli. I said no.

I may have also told him I was vegetarian. I didn't get the job.

I walked back up the hill to my grandmother's house, utterly dejected.

A few days and some more pity parties later, I found a number for a headhunter based in New York City. I called and talked about my experience as a personal assistant to the Director.

Because his was a name that everyone knew, the headhunter agreed to meet me for an interview.

The next day, I took the train into the city and met with the headhunter. She told me she had been looking for an assistant for a "very high-powered female fashion executive." She thought my background might make me a good candidate for the job. I took the information and let her schedule an interview.

Later that week, I found myself on Fifth Avenue for the interview. A week after that, I started as a personal assistant to a woman who ran a fashion empire. I was employed for a total of twelve days.

The moment I met Josie Natori, I knew I was in the presence of greatness.

Similar to how I feel about Albert Finney, I have no

desire to hide her identity. Josie Natori was a 'boss' in the best sense of the word, and she should be celebrated.

Josie was tough, decisive, and unwaveringly serious when it came to her business.

On my first day at work, Josie called me into her office to go through her schedule for the week.

I had arrived early to make a good impression. I jumped up from my desk, grabbed a stack of Post-it notes, and waited for her instructions.

Josie started rambling off her schedule, to the minute, at a breakneck pace. I couldn't write fast enough. I kept filling my Post-it notes. I went through my entire stack before she had made it through one day of things I needed to schedule.

When she finally took a breath, Josie looked up at me. I was standing there, in my olive-green suit from TJ Maxx. Along my left sleeve were thirty Post-it notes. I had subconsciously removed and stuck each note to my arm while Josie talked.

I was standing in front of a fashion legend wearing a cheap suit now adorned with scribbled yellow Post-it notes.

I think it was clear to both of us, in that moment, that I was not cut out to be anyone's personal assistant. Josie needed, and deserved, someone that could organize a calendar. Josie was worthy of someone with the ambition to rise in the fashion world. I couldn't have cared less about fashion. My own, or anyone else's.

It was clear to me that this was a terrible fit. Pun intended.

Still, out of respect and admiration for Josie, for the next ten days, I really tried.

I got to the office an hour before everyone else. I left Josie little notes of affirmation around her office. It hadn't occurred to me that a titan of her industry didn't need a "This is going to be a GREAT day" stuck to her pen holder.

The final straw came on the day that Josie had an early morning interview with a woman named Elsa Klensch. Elsa was the beloved and very well-respected host of a show called "Style with Elsa Klensch" on CNN. I knew that this was a big deal for the company. Everyone in the office was buzzing. I arrived at the office by 6:30 a.m., to set up the coffee, and bagels, and schmears.

Josie called on her way in with a list of things she needed for the meeting. I couldn't make sense of any of it. I had no knowledge of the differences between a fall collection and a spring collection, let alone the difference of a staple in a fashion collection-an item that serves as a core piece of the collection, from the little silver fastener found in a stapler.

I left Josie Natori an encouraging note on her desk, something like "You've GOT this." And I took the 9:00 a.m. bus back to Yonkers.

Dear Josie Natori,

I left you a note on your desk. I hope you found it. I wanted to take a minute to write this letter to you in hopes of further explaining myself. Not that you have any reason to hear me out, or to understand my immature behavior. I am sorry I quit without any notice. There is no excuse for that.

At the risk of this sounding like a breakup letter, I need you to know–it had nothing to do with you, and everything to do with me.

I wish I had the courage to tell you to your face, instead of leaving a note on your desk before your big meeting. But I didn't. I panicked. I was so afraid of letting you down, I let you down even more.

I know you could see that I was entirely in the wrong place. You deserved so much better.

You deserved someone that cares about fashion! It's the industry you have made an indelible mark on. I know there are thousands of women out there that would kill to have had my job.

I just wasn't one of them.

More than anything, I wanted to send this letter to say thank you for the kindness and the patience you showed me.

I am sorry I didn't have the confidence to speak up to you. I would have told you I was a lousy assistant and always would be. I might be a great brand strategist or copy editor, but not an assistant.
I should have told you the moment I knew. Which was immediately.
I also want to tell you that you are an inspiration. I truly admire you.
I have never met anyone before, and I haven't met anyone since, that balances such power with such grace. I remain so impressed by you.
When I look back at my two weeks of working with you, I realize I didn't learn a thing about fashion. Instead, I learned so much about how to be a strong, confident, successful woman.
Thank you, Josie.
Rachel

HINDSIGHT

I love this story. It's like *The Devil Wears Prada,* but with the roles reversed. I was the nightmare, not Josie, the boss.

Even though my entire career working for Josie Natori didn't even last three weeks, I have so many hindsights from that time. I can now see that I should have asked for help. I should have admitted what I didn't know. I should have used my voice to speak up and explain that I really had no formal corporate training and that if Josie needed a traditional assistant, it couldn't be me. In short, when I felt in over my head in the first thirty minutes of working there, I should have said something.

This story also helps me understand there are hundreds of ways in which we can fail to speak up. It doesn't always have to be in response to being overlooked or wronged. Josie was nothing but patient and supportive of me. I failed to speak up and be honest about my *own* shortcomings.

I was afraid to admit what I didn't know and what I couldn't do. And I put myself in a position that wasn't fair to myself, or to Josie.

What is not in the story is what happened after I quit so abruptly that Wednesday morning.

I took the bus back to Yonkers and spent the day in the fetal position while my grandma's house phone rang off the hook. The recruiting agency called a dozen times. I never answered.

That next Monday, the phone rang again, and this time I picked it up. To my dismay, it was the recruiting agency. The woman on the other end of the phone told me she had never seen anything like this in ten years of doing her job. I started to apologize and tell her how embarrassed I was by my behavior. She stopped me. "Not that," she said.

She told me that Mrs. Natori had personally called their office and told them that if I quit because I wasn't happy with my salary or working conditions that she would give me a raise and better hours, effective immediately.

I had walked out on this woman before one of her biggest interviews, and she was calling the agency to see what I needed to come back.

I was stunned.

I didn't go back (I still couldn't care less about fashion), but if I had spoken up, who knows what could have happened? I could have been moved to the marketing department, or somewhere else where I may have thrived. I will never know.

I had an ally in Josie, but I failed to see it. I lacked the confidence and the voice to persevere through my insecurities. I gave up on myself, and in doing so, I gave up the opportunity to work for a powerful, successful woman who believed in me. I didn't realize it at the time, but I would spend the rest of my career searching for exactly this kind of allyship.

ONWARDS

Make a list of women you admire.

If it isn't clear yet, I *love* a list. And I love this Onwards because it is about women.

On my list of women I admire, Josie would be at the top. It's important to find examples of women speaking the fuck up and doing things that are inspiring to you. If you can think of two or three or ten women, write their names down. Seeing their names in front of you will trigger memories or images of them doing something (probably speaking the fuck up!) that you can take energy and strength from.

Just as every Onwards is a suggestion and not an obligation, there are no rules. The women on your list can be living or dead, women you know or women you have never met. Immediately, I think of Ruth Bader Ginsburg, the notorious RBG, and how she should be on every woman's list, but most of us probably haven't had the honor of having met her honor.

The amount of time you spend thinking of your list is just as important as your thoughts about the women on it. Is it easy to make this list? Do you have a plethora of names to choose from and have the luxury of being selective? Or is it hard to come up with any names at all? If the latter is true, let's work on changing that. Together

YOU CAN GO HOME AGAIN

I look back fondly on that short time I spent living with my grandmother in Yonkers, even if we did usually eat dinner on trays in front of the TV while listening to the less-than-mellifluous dings of tiles turned over by the strangely ageless Vanna White.

The consistency and security I felt during that short time healed me. After the heartbreak that was Las Vegas, my time in Yonkers was exactly what I needed.

After failing so miserably in the fashion world of New York City, I didn't have it in me to try for another job, so instead, I went back to my childhood home on Cape Cod.

My mom had fully recovered from her second marriage. She had opened a little art and jewelry store on the main street of town. Besides the brick-and-mortar location, my mom had recently added another element to her business: a website.

A few years before, when I was still living in Los Angeles and cocktail waitressing to pay my bills, my mom had called to tell me about a recent discovery of hers. She asked if I had ever heard of "the World Wide Web."

It was the early aughts, and online shopping was just becoming a thing for most people. My mother had found a company that would build a one-page website for a business. The cost was $150.

My mom decided to go for it.

She had called me in Los Angeles to share the news. She was launching an online jewelry store. She told me I should follow in her footsteps and start my own site for $150.

When I asked her what I would sell on my one-page e-commerce site, my mom did not hesitate for one minute. "Lesbian sex toys," she said.

To this day, I imagine what life would have been like had I taken her advice. My guess is that I would be very, very rich.

When I got back to Cape Cod, my mom was running the small shop and the one-page website. She had never made a sale on the site, but all over the shop she had printed signs. "Be sure to visit us on the World Wide Web!"

To this day, one of my favorite things about my mother is her relentless optimism. (She has the top spot on *my* list of women I admire.)

On the other hand, I wasn't working and didn't have any promising prospects. I started to explore options to enhance her website and perhaps generate some income. I came across a California-based company specializing in building websites for companies. I called them to discuss designing our site, and they quoted me $12,000 to create a complete online store. A curious number today, given the tools we have to build our own websites for free, but at that time, few people possessed the skills or acumen to do it on their own.

My good friend Gail, a successful music producer who lived in Malibu, generously offered to loan me the money. Gail also let me stay at her house while I was working on the website. She told me she had every confidence we would be successful, and that my mom and I could pay her back later once we started making sales.

A few months later, we had a totally functional, multi-page website.

We still didn't have any sales, but both my mom and I felt like we were on the cutting edge of something big.

I hadn't made a conscious decision, I just started running the business. And I jumped in with both feet. I rearranged the gallery and started a newsletter. I had something to focus on and I was grateful for that.

One day, my mom came home from the supermarket with the new issue of *People* magazine. We never read *People* magazine. She explained that one of our jewelry artists was mentioned in the magazine, so she thought we should have a copy. After all, we did own a thirty-dollar laminator for our hand-printed signs, which we could use to laminate the article and display it in this jeweler's case.

We flipped through and found a story about Winona Ryder. Winona had recently bought a bracelet engraved with an inspirational quote. There was an inset photo of the bracelet. "Cool," I said and went back to work.

Mom called the artist to congratulate her, and we forgot about the article.

The next morning, Mom burst into the gallery while I was setting up.

She shouted that we had over two hundred orders on our website. People had seen the article and went online to find the bracelet. We were the only place on the internet selling them.

This was how our online business started. We grew from one artist to one hundred and fifty.

We marketed ourselves as the place for "Jewelry with Meaning."

Many of the pieces we sold could also be found at Barneys, Neiman Marcus, and Nordstrom, at double the price. We offered free shipping and always sent a personal note with every order. I had a rule that no matter how small the order, the package would include a handwritten thank-you. There were days when the only thing I did was write these thank-you notes.

For the first time since my mom opened the brick-and-mortar gallery, we had to hire people to help. Four women came on full-time to fulfill the orders we were receiving. Over the holidays, we would hire even more help to handle the demand.

We converted the lower level of the gallery into a shipment center.

During this boom time, there was a routine to all my days. I would get into the office by five in the morning to have a few hours to myself. I would print orders, lay out the jewelry, and write the thank-you notes. When the staff came in at nine, I would have everything set up and ready to go for them.

Although my days were long, I was happy during this time. I finally had something to devote myself to. I could channel my love of structure, my work ethic, and my focus into this business.

For almost five years, we were incredibly successful. We sold millions of dollars' worth of jewelry. We kept our overhead low. There were magazine and television stories about our thriving mother–daughter business.

When the recession of 2008 hit, our small business was especially vulnerable. We couldn't keep up with the changing way that people shopped. Platforms like Etsy, and later, eBay and Amazon, began to take a significant portion of our customer base.

When I talk about my career trajectory in job interviews, I tend to leave this part of my working life out, or I downplay it. Perhaps because it came on the tail end of my first attempt at working in New York City, which I deemed a massive failure. Despite our incredible success operating our business out of East Sandwich, Massachusetts, I thought I would be judged for my inability to make it in the big city.

You better believe there is a hindsight about this.

Creating the online company with my mother was the most career success I have ever had. And it should not be discounted. And not just because we made a lot of money. More important than being financially successful, the company we built together positively affected people's lives.

I could write another book about what I experienced selling jewelry online to women.

Allow me to explain.

Jewelry shopping differs from shopping for other items. In most cases, buying the most popular, trendy, or coveted jewelry does not require having a specific weight or body measurement. And by shopping online, women could browse and buy from the safety of their homes.

During my five years running the company, more than a dozen women confided in me that they were agoraphobic. Many more shared issues with their weight, their husband's infidelity, their frustration around not advancing at work. Because our company mostly sold jewelry with inspiring quotes engraved or stamped into them, women were primarily buying our pieces as talismans. They were buying our jewelry to serve as signifiers of strength, hope, or resilience.

I also learned that many women found comfort in shopping for our pieces while they were undergoing chemotherapy treatments for cancer. Because we took such a personal approach to our company and sent handwritten thank-you notes, many women felt comfortable opening up to us. They would send emails or mail letters. Over the course of five years, I corresponded with hundreds of our customers. And many of them told me their stories.

A shockingly high percentage of our female customers wrote and told me they were battling cancer. Many said they found our website because they were looking for a piece of jewelry to make them feel brave.

I was so touched that these women shared their stories with me. I wanted to do something for them. In addition to having many pen pals, I wrote two small books during this time, entitled *How to Avoid Being Sad* Volumes 1 and 2. I also started painting on paint sample cards from Home Depot, calling them "tiny revolutions."

Both the books and the paintings were small, unpolished things, but I enjoyed sending them as gifts to our customers.

What happened next will forever be a favorite memory of mine.

Dozens of these women came together to send me a thank-you gift. One customer organized a shipment of Christmas presents to me from over forty of our customers.

This same group, along with some others, started calling themselves "The Girls of Giving Tree." (Our gallery was called the Giving Tree after my favorite book as a child.)

This group would plan trips and outings together. I had nothing to do with the organizing of these in-person meetings.

Following the closure of the gallery and website due to the recession, I came to discover that these women had also organized support trips to visit others in the group who were undergoing chemotherapy treatments. I had no idea of the deep connection these women had forged, or the support and strength they were able to give to each other, specifically because they understood one another's struggles.

I will remain forever in awe and hold deep respect for the community these women built and the unwavering support they provided for one another.

The irony of what would eventually become my career isn't lost on me. In the next decade I would immerse myself in the membership club space, striving to create loyal and devoted communities. However, out of all the clubs I established, none of the meticulously organized and manufactured communities could ever hold a candle to the Girls of Giving Tree.

Dear Girls of Giving Tree,

Thank you.

I am crying again while writing a letter, only this time they are tears of awe, of being so moved thinking of the kindness that exists in this world.

I have never written a letter to all of you together.

Many of you have those two little books, How to Avoid Being Sad Volumes 1 and 2.

I wrote them for all of you.

You all were not only the first customers of our business, you were also the first people that read my writing.

For our five years in business, you were loyal to our company. You also showed me, personally, so much kindness. I was lonely during that time. But you found me. You all always let me know that I wasn't alone.

After we closed, I heard you found one another too.

I learned that a group of you traveled together to support

Nancy during her chemotherapy. I heard that when Carol died, many of you went to Houston to attend her funeral.
I've only ever met a few of you in person.
I heard your group grew to over one hundred women. What an incredible feat!
I am sorry I didn't stay in touch after we closed the gallery.
I think I needed to take some time to heal.
I know that you know I put my entire heart and soul into that business.
Some of my favorite memories are of receiving your emails and letters.
I want to take a moment to send one back and tell you what a difference you made in my life.
You are all incredible, remarkable women.
Not to end on a sad note, but we found out this year that Mom has stage four cancer.
It's in her brain, and her lungs and liver and bones.
I want all of you to know that I am taking so much strength from all of you.
Even though it has been years since the Giving Tree Gallery was open, I think about all of you, the "Girls of Giving Tree," all the time.
I have no doubt you stay in touch with each other.
Will you all say a prayer for Mom?
I have seen the power of what that can do, coming from all of you.
Thank you.
Yours, always,
Rachel

HINDSIGHT

Though this story may not at first appear to directly align with the overarching theme of learning how to speak the fuck up, it becomes relevant the moment I recognized that I needed to speak the fuck up to the voice in my head that told me that the life I was living was "not enough."

I am sad and embarrassed that I wasn't always *so proud* of this time in my career. I get so angry with myself for spending years thinking that because it didn't happen in some big city, in some shiny office, that it didn't count.

I hate that I once thought living with my mom as an adult and co-creating a beautiful business with her amounted to a personal failure and wasn't deserving of my pride.

Waitressing was my favorite job, and I decided it wasn't "good enough" to be a career.

Owning and operating the Giving Tree Gallery was such a rewarding and enriching experience, and yet I deemed it small.

I missed the forest for the trees.

I judged myself. I let other people's standards of what success should look like tarnish the success and joy I found in both waitressing and running the gallery.

I let the voice in my head keep me from the truth I knew in my heart.

This story also makes me question where I was getting my ideas about success.

From a purely financial perspective, my time at the Giving Tree was my most successful.

When I was waitressing, I easily afforded my rent and any fancy dinner I wanted to treat myself to. During both times in my life, I was completely debt-free. And I was happy.

Why didn't I see that as a resounding success?

Now that my mom is sick, I would give anything, absolutely *anything,* to go back to this time when we were spending every day together. When she was full of life and radiance, even if she was a bit too enthusiastic about laminating a sign.

I know this hindsight will be all too familiar to anyone that is living with the constant fear of losing the person they love the most in this world, but it is worth stating here.

Spending time with people you love is the greatest gift this journey of life holds. It is time spent that you will never regret, and time you will never get back.

Do it now.

ONWARDS

TRUST YOUR OWN JOY.

Another all-caps Onwards. And there is a greater than sixty percent chance this phrase will be my next tattoo.

Make this phrase a meditation. Close your eyes and say this over and over to yourself. Four tiny words that together are indescribably powerful.

"Trust Your Own Joy."

"Trust Your Own Joy."

"Trust Your Own Joy."

The more I repeat these four words, the less I feel the need to elaborate.

It's all there, isn't it? These four words together say it all.

Bonus Onwards: Get this tattoo.

Just kidding. Or maybe not!

Start a journal entry with this question:

What would I do if other people's opinions didn't matter to me?

It's a really fun question. If you were free of judgment, from yourself *and* others, how would you really want to spend your days?

As with all Onwards, there are no rules and no wrong answers.

I have a deep longing to work in a coffee shop. And I hope to fulfill that dream someday. Whenever I return to the car with my oat milk latte from Dunkin' Donuts (which is four dollars cheaper than Starbucks), I invariably tell Jenna that I want to quit my career and start working there.

It's not just the appealing hours (beginning at six a.m. and finishing at one p.m., leaving the rest of the day free) that attract me. Serving strong coffee and sweet treats seems like it would bring a lot of joy and be a lot of fun. I love picturing myself sending off the construction crew, the schoolteacher, and the firefighter with a coffee, a donut, and a smile each morning.

I want to make it clear that I hold absolutely no judgment around this kind of work. What I do question is why the salaries for honest jobs like this are so far below the bloated salaries of *so* many antiquated C-suite positions- people doing so little work except making rich people richer, but not making anyone's day a little brighter, the way a smile and a donut can do.

Thinking about what you would do if other people's opinions didn't matter allows your mind to expand to accommodate different kinds of happiness. Happiness that is authentic to you.

Doing this exercise in the context of learning how to speak the fuck up starts to reframe your current experiences. You can start to look at things you may be doing that you actually don't want to do, and you can start to ask yourself why.

This isn't advice to quit your job. It is simply saying that when you can start imagining a scenario where you make your own rules, you can start to understand the times when you are deferring to someone else's. You can begin to realize that your struggle to find your voice or to be heard is often tied to engaging in actions that are outside your true-truth about what really makes you happy

THE WORST PERSON IN THE WORLD

For the five years that my mother and I had the online business, I was entirely focused on growing the company. I enjoyed being at work before dawn and working into the evening. I moved into a nearby beach house the owners rented in the winter months and my nights were spent with my loyal and cherished companion, my dog Beazie, who was my best friend.

Every night after work, Beazie and I would visit the beach and discuss what we should make for dinner. There was a fish market a mile away that we would walk to and pick up our ingredients.

One Friday night, I had finished cleaning up dinner and settled into bed to read a book. It was just past eight.

My phone rang, waking me up. I answered groggily.

It was my friend Cassie, a painter who was living in New York City.

"What are you doing?!" she asked me.

"I guess I was sleeping?" I said, more as a question than an answer, realizing I must have fallen asleep while reading.

Cassie was having *none* of it.

"You are thirty-five years old! In the prime of your life! And it's a Friday night!"

Cassie went on to tell me I was dangerously close to what she called "old recluse shut off from the world" territory. She told me that I had to put a stop to this behavior immediately.

She insisted I plan to come to New York City to see her the very next weekend. I made her a halfhearted promise and went back to sleep

A few days after Cassie's call, I got a voice message from an old customer of mine at Shutters. It was from a man that had been a fixture on various TV shows for many years.

Let's call him TV man.

I hadn't heard from TV man in a few years. When I had waited on him at Shutters, he would always linger at one of my tables late into the afternoon. Like Albert Finney, he was someone that would stay at Shutters for weeks on end while he was filming something in Los Angeles. I had a hard time imagining his work schedule because he always seemed to be in the lobby lounge, with nothing to do, when I started my normal shift at two p.m.

From his attention, I might have suspected that TV man was hitting on me, but he never made a move. When I told him I was gay, he asked questions with what felt like genuine interest and reflected his intellectual curiosity. TV man was known for being very smart. He had made a career broadcasting his erudite insights about a wide variety of topics, from sports to politics and technology. TV man was like a walking Wikipedia. He seemed to know a little, or more than a little, about everything.

While TV man had questions about my sexuality, he described himself as asexual. He said he didn't have time, and he wasn't interested, in dating.

I enjoyed our conversations and we struck up a friendship. He would discuss global events and current affairs, while I would regale him with stories about my weekly excursions to a place called "Girl Bar" in West Hollywood. I would tell him what drama I had stirred up, and because of it, who I was currently entangled with.

For months at a time when TV man was working in Los Angeles we would have almost daily chats in the lobby lounge of Shutters.

Whenever TV man had to return New York, he would find me to say goodbye. Besides occasionally tuning in on television, I didn't see TV man again.

So, when I received his voice mail more than seven years later, I was genuinely surprised.

I called him back and we talked for an hour. TV man told me he was having quite a hard go of it lately. He explained that he had lost his mother six months ago. Then his father, who had gone to the hospital for something routine some weeks ago, had also unexpectedly passed.

I remembered from our conversations in LA that TV man had never married and had no children.

During our phone call, he sounded not just sad, but also quite lost.

TV man told me he had come across my number and had been thinking about how I had always managed to make him feel better when he was having a shitty day in LA. He said he thought by calling me now, I might be able to do the same thing.

When I told TV man I was thinking of coming to New York in a few days, he asked if we could meet in person.

That next weekend, before I saw Cassie, I met TV man for a walk around Central Park.

My sense during the phone call had been correct.

With the death of both of his parents, it felt like TV man was questioning his own existence.

It felt to me like he was having an existential crisis, along with suffering a deep depression.

When I asked him about marriage and children, he got cagey. He said he had recently gone through a bad breakup. His ex was a much younger woman in the same industry. When he spoke of her, TV man appeared emotionally heightened and dysregulated.

That afternoon, I mostly just listened. To stories about his parents, his work, his struggle to find meaning in anything.

After a few hours of sitting on a park bench, I told him I had to meet Cassie, who was forcing me to attend an art gallery dinner.

He asked if I could stay in New York for a while, to spend some time with him.

I explained that my business wasn't doing well and

that I didn't have any money to spend on a place to stay in New York.

We hugged and I went to my dinner.

Cassie had warned me that the dinner was just an excuse. She told me she was playing matchmaker for me. Her friend Spencer, who owned a gallery on the Upper East Side, knew a woman they both had agreed would be perfect for me.

Spencer was hosting the dinner, and the woman would be there. Cassie gave me vague details in the cab to the Upper East Side. Her name was Helena, and she was a gallerist living in Chelsea.

We arrived at the dinner, and Spencer introduced me to Helena. I immediately felt out of my depth, but I was intrigued. I can't say it was the same for her. Helena spent about seven seconds talking to me before disappearing for the rest of the evening.

TV man called me early the next morning and asked me to meet him for coffee at the café below his Trump Tower apartment. When I arrived, instead of ordering coffee, TV man asked if he could take me upstairs and show me something. We stopped off at his penthouse, where he retrieved a set of keys, and then took the elevator down a few floors.

After we got off the elevator, TV man unlocked the door to a giant one-bedroom apartment. Light streamed in through the floor-to-ceiling windows. The apartment was entirely empty except for a hospital bed in the middle of the room.

TV man stood next to the bed and told me he had recently bought the apartment for his father after his surgery, and now he had no use for it.

He said he wasn't ready to sell it, so he had the thought I could stay there, if I wanted.

I was stunned. This offer came as a total surprise.

I thought about the wonderful time I'd had the evening before. I loved the gallery dinner. I loved the energy of being around so many creative and smart people. Being in New York for just one night had reminded me of how much I was missing. For months on the Cape, my only evening conversations had been with my dog.

And with the recession still going strong, my business was imploding. It was becoming increasingly hard to bear witness to. So, although strange and surreal, what TV man was proposing was also exciting, and remarkably well timed.

Having learned a bit from the situation in California years ago, I asked a few questions.

Would I have to pay rent? No. Did he want to live with me? No! He had his own place; this was just a waste of an apartment at this point. Could I do anything to help him in exchange for the apartment? TV man paused for a moment and then proposed that I could "remind him to eat before he left for work." If I was shopping for groceries for myself, I could pick up the Special K with berries that he liked. And if I had free time on weekends, he would like to go to some baseball games. He mentioned that there was nothing specific that he had in mind.

I decided that what TV man was really needing was a friend. I accepted his offer.

I drove a small U-Haul of things to New York City that next week. Some small furniture items, all my favorite art and clothes, my bicycle, and my computer. Just the things I cared about most. I bought a couch online but couldn't afford to also buy a bed, so as weird as it was, I slept on the hospital bed.

If it sounds a bit macabre, it's because it was.

When I was settled in New York into what I guess was my new Upper East Side apartment, I went to visit Helena at her gallery. I asked her if she would consider having dinner with me.

She agreed, and we made a date for the next week.

Before that happened, I spent a Saturday holed up in my new apartment, drinking a bottle of rosé and then one of tequila with a jewelry artist acquaintance of mine. My mom and I had carried her work on our website, and although I knew she was straight, I'd always had a massive crush on her. When she kissed me on the floor of my empty apartment late that afternoon, I truly felt like I was winning life's lottery.

I stood up, took her hand, and led her to the hospital bed.

The next day, nursing a hangover, I met TV man at an outdoor café around the corner and we had a leisurely brunch. I told him all about the dalliance with my long-time crush, and I pouted into my coffee about how almost immediately afterward, she had started talking about her boyfriend.

A few days later, I had my date with Helena. Within the first twenty minutes, I knew I wanted to spend a lot more time with her. And I did.

We started seeing each other often. I learned early on in our courtship that owning an art gallery in Chelsea, New York, and owning one in East Sandwich, Massachusetts, were *very* different things.

Despite being so mismatched, we genuinely enjoyed each other's company. After about a month of dating, we knew we were falling in love.

Because Helena had a young daughter, she wanted to be thoughtful about how she would introduce me to her. She told me she closed her gallery for a month in the summer, and would I consider spending it with the two of them in the Hamptons? Helena said she thought this would be the perfect way for her daughter to get to know me and feel comfortable with me being around.

I was ecstatic. I could hardly wait to tell TV man that I was in love. I hadn't told him about Helena because he had started hosting another show and was always on edge or exhausted, and we were only seeing each other about once a week for a baseball game or a meal.

(I would learn later that he was fighting an opioid addiction, which explained his mood swings and strange behavior.)

When I went to his apartment with a box of Special K, he seemed to be in a particularly bad mood. He invited me in, and I proceeded to tell him all about Helena, her daughter, and our plan to spend a month in the Hamptons.

What happened next was as surprising as anything that has ever happened to me.

TV man lost his shit.

I have never seen anything like the rage I saw on his face. TV man started screaming at me about how close he was to proposing marriage to me, and how we were supposed to have children and that I was supposed to be *his wife*.

I was dumbfounded. TV man knew I was gay from the moment I met him so many years ago. I had told him about the women I was dating or hooking up in hospital beds with.

Our relationship wasn't romantic or sexual in any way. And we certainly weren't in a place to get married. My brain tried to compute—could TV man possibly have thought that we were dating this entire time? As I tried to cut through my fog of confusion, another feeling overtook me. One of terror.

TV man was over 6 feet tall and easily 250 pounds. He was hovering over me, inches from my face, spit running down his chin. He was bright red with rage. He was shouting and shoving his finger in my face. Over and over, TV man insisted that he was planning to propose, and I had ruined everything.

I backed out of his apartment and rushed down fourteen flights of stairs. I didn't even stop back at my apartment. I went straight to Helena's and spent the night.

The next morning, I waited until I knew TV man would be gone to film his show before I returned to the apartment complex.

I walked into the giant, garish, marble lobby and saw the doorman, Bobby.

I started to say hello when Bobby stopped me.

"I am sorry, Ms. Smith, but I am not allowed to let you enter the building."

"Excuse me?"

"I am sorry, Ms. Smith, but Mr. TV man has informed us that you cannot enter the building."

I asked Bobby what was going on. I told him that everything I owned—my clothes, my bicycle, my computer with all my work and writing on it—was in that apartment.

"I'm sorry."

I asked if I could have two minutes to just get my computer. He could come with me.

"I'm sorry."

I asked if he could go get it.

"Mr. TV man has said that no one is to enter the apartment."

I called TV man a dozen times, but he never answered.

I sent emails, and for months I begged him to just let me have my stuff back.

He never returned a single message.

I read on Page Six of the *New York Post* that TV man had signed one of the largest single network hosting contracts in history. A guaranteed $40 million.

A few months later, news about his addiction would also appear in this same newspaper. TV man started a public downward spiral and was fired. I read that the network was forced to pay TV man even more money just to get rid of him.

Dear TV man,

Did it make you feel better to take everything I owned from me?

You had forty million dollars in your bank account. I had four hundred, and yet it felt necessary to you to keep every possession I cared about? My computer with my years of writing?

And why? Because I hurt your ego?

I told you I was in love with a woman. (Because. I. Am. Gay.)

And you made this about me rejecting you?

Did you think that because you were "going to propose to me" that of course I would say yes? That it didn't matter that I was gay?

TV man—We never kissed. We never had sex. We never even went on a romantic date. But I was going to say yes to marrying you?

Because I am me, a woman without agency or autonomy, and you are you—a big-deal TV man?

Is your ego really that big, or are you delusional?
In your mind, I was staying in that apartment downstairs until I married you and I moved upstairs.
What you were actually doing was holding me hostage in that apartment. Did you even see me as an actual human being, or was I just an object to you?
After your doorman informed me I was never going to be able to get any of my things, I desperately wanted to call Page Six. You were already somewhat of a darling of theirs; this would have made headlines for sure.
I didn't do it.
I didn't publicly call you out when I could have, when I should have, because I knew there would be fallout and I didn't want to ruin you. I remained your friend even when you completely abandoned our friendship.
That has ended now.
What is ironic is that at the same time as my awful experience with you, I did find a love of my life, who will forever be one of the best things to ever happen to me.
I am quite positive you have not had the same good fortune.
I understand now that because you are so afraid of being discovered as a fraud, because you are so cripplingly insecure and feel deep down that you are unworthy of love, that you terrorize everyone around you.
You do this to feel better about yourself.
But it's not working, is it?
You took my physical possessions from me, but you are the one left with nothing.
You are bereft.
Now, you have lost your only friend.
You are not the "worst person in the world", but you are not a good one.
And you will be a very lonely one.
As you TV hosts say:
Goodnight, and good luck.
Rachel

HINDSIGHTS

I hate this story with a passion that is hard to put into words. I didn't include this story in the first draft of this book because it feels so nonsensical and surreal. But it happened, and it is a bridge from one phase of my life into another, so I decided to include it.

It's not a story about a time in my career. It's about what happened when I moved to New York City in my thirties. TV man wasn't my boss, but there was still an incredibly imbalanced power dynamic based on economics. I was in a vulnerable position because suddenly this man controlled not my livelihood, but my access to safe shelter.

I never should have moved into that apartment. A big part of the reason I did was because I believed I was doing TV man a favor. I thought that having me close, and having a friend, would help keep him from hurting so much. That was my justification.

It was a gorgeous apartment in New York City. For free.

Nothing like that is free.

I now see that I was pulling the wool over my own eyes.

But that doesn't mean I am to blame.

I really struggled with the hindsights for this story. For a long time, I left this section blank.

Throughout the writing process, Jenna would read everything and we would discuss it.

We had so many conversations around the hindsight for this story. I tried a dozen times to find it.

I compared it to what happened in Las Vegas. In that instance, I learned the importance of consistently acting in one's self-interest and prioritizing self-protection. In that story, I needed to speak the fuck up by asking questions and checking sources.

With TV man, it's not that I wasn't looking out for myself or that I failed to protect myself. We had always had an enjoyable friendship, and he had shared so much vulnerability with me about how he felt lost after his parents' death. I felt safe. I thought I *was* safe.

In a later story I can so clearly see a hindsight about needing to learn how to create boundaries for myself.

For this story, I kept coming up empty.

And then I realized, maybe *that* is the hindsight. And that is why this story needed to be included.

I couldn't find the hindsight because there really isn't one.

I don't always have to reexamine every situation a hundred times to see where I could have been louder, more assertive, and more confident.

Sometimes, people are just assholes. The work isn't mine to do.

TV man is an asshole.

There are still articles about his outbursts and fits of rage. He is frequently called a bully in the media.

What feels best for the hindsight section of this story is to stop spending any more time trying to write it. What feels best is to just walk away.

Just like I did from an apartment that still had all my stuff in it.

If a place doesn't feel good to you, if a person doesn't feel good for you, if you don't feel like they are honoring your highest, best interests with their behavior, walk away.

A hindsight after all.

ONWARDS

Breathe through you anger-energy.

I clearly have confusion and anger left over from this story. I can feel it right now as I type these words.

There is a punk song I remember from the nineties: "Rise" by Public Image Ltd. There is a line in the song—"Anger is an energy." I am thinking of that song now.

In my body, this anger-energy is skittish and jumpy. It feels like my anxiety, but it is harder, and it has more spikes.

If you are this far into the book, you are on this journey too. And if there were things in these stories that triggered your own memories, you may feel angry too.

Or maybe you are going through something in real time, right now, that stirs up feelings of anger in you.

This Onwards is for those feelings. For your anger-energy.

I am now going to do the single thing that tops my "Pet peeves of things people say" list. When someone tells me to "breathe," it makes me want to scream.

I always want to shout, "Me, breathe? How about *you* breathe!"

I hate being told to breathe.

But ten times out of ten, when someone tells me to do it, it is because I need to do it.

It is because I am angry.

For this Onwards, find a comfortable, quiet space.

Sit with your hands resting on your belly.

After you read this, close your eyes, and start.

Start to breathe, in through your nose and out through your mouth.

Take a breath in that lasts for four seconds and a breath out that lasts for eight.

Breathe from your belly and not your chest. Use your hands to guide your attention to the rising and falling of your belly.

Breathe.

As you breathe, think of emptying out your body of the anger-energy it is holding. Feel that energy coming to the surface with your inhale and then releasing out of you on the exhale.

Do this for as long as it takes to feel your heart settle and slow. Do this until you have released the anger-energy you were feeling.

Onwards.

A CULTURE OF SEX AND COMPLICITY

I left TV man's apartment and went on to have a wonderful summer with Helena and her daughter. After a month in the Hamptons, Helena invited me to move in with the two of them in Chelsea.

One evening, Helena arrived home from work and told me she had received a call to serve on a membership committee. The call came from a woman named Katherine, who was the membership director for a swanky private members' club. Katherine was bringing together influential people in New York City to grow the club's membership base.

I knew the club Helena was talking about. It was only a few blocks from our apartment, but it was not a place I would have ever thought of or wanted to go. I told Helena as much.

I made quite a fuss about how elitist I found the concept of private membership clubs. I told her that only insecure people desperate for approval would need to join a place like the one she was talking about.

Helena patiently listened while I went on my rant.

And then, just as calmly, she said, "I already said yes."

Helena was always open to opportunities that might put her in the path of new collectors for her gallery. Plus, she explained, they hosted the committee for dinners.

At worst, it's a free dinner, she rationalized.

This conversation with Helena was typical. She would always humor my opinions and outbursts, but she would always do things her way. Approximately ninety-nine percent of the time, Helena would be right.

Helena went to her committee dinner and had a wonderful time. She came home that night and told me just how wrong I had been. She said she enjoyed everyone she met and didn't find the club at all "douchey," as I had taken to calling it.

Helena told me that at dinner, Katherine had announced that she would be leaving her position in a month. She had asked the group if they had any recommendations for someone to replace her as the membership director.

Helena told me she submitted my name for consideration.

After another outburst, I calmed down enough to ask questions.

How on earth was I qualified to be a membership director, having never been to a private club in my life?

Helena told me that didn't matter. She said that I just needed to be a "people person," which I was. She said that if I impressed the owner of the company, I would have a good chance of getting the job.

A week later, I had been through two in-person interviews and was set up with a Zoom meeting to talk to the owner, who was based in London.

I remember the Zoom call perfectly. It was me, an Englishman who was the global head of membership, and the owner of the company.

I was not used to taking Zoom meetings. When the meeting started and the two men joined, I was unsure if I could be heard clearly. At the start of the video, I could be seen moving my head up and down. I was trying to figure out how far to be from the microphone.

The owner joked that if I just kept doing that for the entire Zoom call, I would absolutely get the job.

The sexual nature of that comment completely derailed me.

I had flashbacks to working for the Director. Everything had sexual undertones. And if they didn't have undertones, they had explicit overtones. There was no mistaking what the club owner meant.

I tried to hide my shock. This happened thirty seconds into my job interview, and after a "nice to meet you," it was the first thing the owner of the company said to me.

I took a deep breath and continued the interview, trying to hide how totally discombobulated I was.

I must have done okay because I got the job.

My start date corresponded with the opening day of a large art fair in New York. The membership club was hosting a pop-up lounge at the fair. The owner had flown in from London to attend. My first assignment was to spend the day hosting members in the pop-up lounge.

The executive team wanted me to introduce myself to as many members as I could.

It was an important day for me on many levels: It was my first day at a new job. I was determined to make a great first impression with the owner, the all-male executive team, and the members.

I barely slept the night before.

I met the owner, the COO, and the CFO at the entrance to the club at eight in the morning. We piled into an SUV to drive to the art fair. Besides these men and the driver, the only other person in the car was an interior designer who worked for the company, a woman named Sylvie. She wasn't considered an executive, but they were bringing her along to oversee the furniture installation at the pop-up.

I was sitting quietly in the back seat of the car, feeling nervous and excited.

The owner turned around from the front passenger seat and called my name. I sat up straight and smiled.

The owner said, "I have a very important question I've been meaning to ask you."

This was my chance. I was going to nail *whatever* he asked.

Then the owner asked me this question.

"In your personal experience, in all your years of research . . . what percentage of the women that you've slept with, you know, gay women . . . lesbians, have been fully shaved?"

I was speechless. My mind started to race at a million miles an hour while every inch of my body broke into a sweat. In five seconds, I did an hour's worth of calculating. The owner knew I had heard about the job from my female partner I lived with. So he knew I was gay. I thought back to his comment on the Zoom call, and how he had sexualized me within three seconds of meeting me. I opened my mouth to speak, but no words came out.

Sylvie, the designer, was sitting next to me, and she was the only person in the car not laughing and staring at me intently.

I realized she was saying something over and over under her breath but so the owner could hear. She kept saying "HR."

She was telling him to stop.

The owner waved his hand as if to shoo off the warning.

He pressed on. "How many?"

I think I sort of blacked out. I cannot for the life of me remember exactly what I said, except, "I don't know," followed by some nonsensical muttering until we pulled into the fairgrounds.

This happened in the very first hour of my very first day at my new job. My first real, adult, working-for-someone-else, living in New York City, job.

During my time at the company, the culture of promiscuity and the casual attitude toward sex were some of the defining characteristics of the brand. It felt like nothing was off limits, and the rumor mill was constantly churning. Everyone knew everything about each other's sex lives.

I pride myself on being a discreet and private person, but when I started dating someone new, a well-known musician, it was like a memo went out to all the executives.

I was constantly asked about our relationship. The owner and the other male executives knew who I was dating. And they would ask questions. My relationship, and as a byproduct, my sexuality, was trotted out at meetings and our annual executive retreat in London. People wanted to know everything. It was as if they felt that it was their right to know everything about my sex life.

In my five years at the company, I excelled. I credit this to my work ethic and the way I treated everyone I worked with. I prided myself on being an approachable, sensitive boss and a strong leader to my teams.

If I had worked somewhere else, I believe my attitude, accomplishments, and success would have ushered in all sorts of career growth. Instead, I was constantly being told how invaluable I was, but that I was already at the highest level for my position.

I can't help but wonder if the hypersexualized culture of the place didn't *also* create a culture that failed to respect women. In the five years I was there, and the ten years since, not a single woman has achieved a C-level executive position at the company.

Because I was gay, I wasn't usually identified as a potential target for the male executives, married or not, when they came to town. But so many of my female colleagues were. For me, and all the women at the company, not a single day went by that we didn't have to, in some way, navigate around a sexual comment or innuendo, a question or proposition.

Frankly, it was exhausting.

Dear Membership Club Owner,

Did you know that working for you was the first real job I've ever had? I mean, I've worked my whole life, I've waitressed for years, I worked on $100 million film sets in Hollywood, I even ran my own company (successfully, mind you), but working for you was the first job I've had that felt totally real.

And it was in New York City. This felt like the stuff of "dreams come true." The stuff that Kate Hudson stars in movies about.

I really thought I had stumbled my way into a career.

I should have known during our first interaction when you suggested that my movements, which looked like giving you a blow job, could have immediately gotten me hired.

I should have known to run then. To run and never look back. But I didn't.

Because I thought of this as a "real" job, I believed the rules would be real too.
It turns out there weren't any rules. Well, not for you and the other male executives. Not for any of you.
And I need you to know that because of this, I never felt safe working at your company.
There wasn't one day that I felt safe.
Because my girlfriend at the time nominated me for the job, you knew I was gay when you hired me. I took comfort in the fact that I didn't have to hide that.
I didn't think it was something that would be brought up, almost every day, and be the main subject of conversation every time I saw you.
My sexuality was a novelty for you and the other men in the company. It was a thing to be snickered and fantasized about. Beyond whispers and smirks, you all felt comfortable talking about it out loud, and to me, all the time.
That question you asked me on my first day should never have been asked.
Nor should you have behaved the way you did whenever the three of you came to town.
You would land from London late in the evening, already many drinks in, and sit at the bar and assess the female members there.
You would call me over and try to get my opinion—on their bodies, their availability, how freaky they would be in bed. You would ask me who I had slept with or who I wanted to.
I felt constantly sexualized. Every time I came into contact with you.
My being gay was a part of your entertainment.
You did the same thing to the gay men at the company.
I know we were some of your best employees. But we could never escape being framed and defined by our sexuality.
I can't imagine any straight man would have ever had to learn how to work around this.
Did you ever have to navigate this in your career?
Were you ever asked a question that was so shockingly inappropriate, so incredibly violating, that you felt like

you were standing there naked, being gawked at, and fearing for your safety?
I highly doubt it.
You know how hard I worked for you, and how much I accomplished.
I was tireless in the energy I gave to helping build your company to the multibillion-dollar success story it is today.
If I had worked somewhere else, I would still be there, rewarded for my efforts.
Instead, I'm writing you this letter to say that the environment you had the heaviest hand in creating for your employees was not safe. And it wasn't fair.
I understand now that you never saw me as someone who could advance to an executive position equal to or above the other men in the company because you were too busy imagining me under another woman.
This truth is a bitter pill I've had to swallow.
But I never should have had to.
This should have never been the reality of what it was to work for you.
Rachel

HINDSIGHTS

This story reveals how things are rarely just black or white, or all good or all bad.

In many ways, this part of my career was one of my most prosperous, and one of my favorites.

So many great things happened for me at this point in my working life, and at this place. I was given the opportunity to grow into my position and thrive in a career I had never even considered. I was able to earn respect and authority for the first time in my professional life, outside of working for myself.

It was only through writing this book and reexamining all my work experiences to uncover the forces that prevented me from speaking the fuck up, that I revealed some true-truths I could no longer ignore.

When I speak of the environment not being "safe," that feels extreme to me, and I debated using the word. Because it was all so subtle. Most of the time, it was an undercurrent of being sexualized, of being the token lesbian, of the casualness around sex, that ultimately contributed to me not feeling safe.

Still, it's not black and white.

The other difficult true-truth in this story is my own level of complicity in the culture of the place because I didn't speak the fuck up. I allowed things to continue as they had always been. I felt unsafe because I didn't do enough to protect myself.

I didn't set boundaries.

For ninety percent of the time, this wasn't an issue. The ten percent of the time when the executive team came to New York from London, it was. I lost my voice.

When these men came to town, instead of focusing on leading my teams, my job was to cater to them. It was up to me to ensure they were always having the best time. The executive team would land at seven in the evening, and we would have a team dinner in the club at eight.

That dinner was a part of my job.

Had I set a boundary for myself, it would have ended there.

When the owner insisted that I carry on the evening with the group of them, taking them to the newest hot spots, organizing a second dinner of Peking duck on the Lower East Side at three in the morning, everyone drunk and sloppy—that wasn't a part of my job.

I should have set a boundary. I should have said no.

These men would disarm me of my autonomy. Without saying a word, they made it abundantly clear that everyone there was working for them, that they made the rules, and they called the shots.

This power dynamic exists in just about every corporate culture in the world.

Often, women bear the additional strain of having to navigate around being sexualized.

This was the dynamic I faced every time these men came to town.

I was so eager to be the best that I sacrificed what was good for my own well-being. I didn't speak up about the things that were off the table and off limits for the work environment.

The environment of this club was not a safe or protective space. I should have kept myself safe from it. I loved my job; I didn't want to quit my job. But I could have established boundaries for myself.

Unlike the last story, the hindsights of this story are clear to me.

- I didn't set boundaries, and I allowed the culture of casual and open conversation around sex to continue.
- I remained silent in a culture that treated sex and sexuality as something to be shared and discussed. My silence was a form of complicity.
- I allowed my sexuality, my being single or being gay, to be a part of my identity at work.

Along with always telling the truth in my stories, I want to take responsibility when I should. And this is one of those times.

ONWARDS

See the subtle.

It took a lot for me to get through that last story and the hindsights.

I even questioned including this story because there was so much positive in the experience.

I came to genuinely like and admire the club owner and I know he respected me as well, in his way. As I wrote and rewrote this story, I started to *see the subtle.*

I started to see the less obvious but very powerful dynamics that made the environment so problematic.

Is there a situation you are in that on the surface looks good and safe, or a person that seems only beneficent, but for some reason you aren't feeling quite right?

Is there anything else going on that could be working to compromise or threaten you?

It is not easy to see the subtle, but it is essential in this journey.

If you can see the subtle, you will start to discover the reasons you may not be speaking the fuck up, and why you must.

Create your own culture.

As I've been writing this book, I've found myself thinking a lot about the passage from the Serenity Prayer by Reinhold Niebuhr that is often recited at Alcoholics Anonymous meetings: "God, grant me the serenity to accept the things I cannot change, the courage to change the things I can, and the wisdom to know the difference."

I have been thinking about the things I can't control, and the things I can.

There are so many dynamics, *subtle* and not, that we experience as women in a patriarchal world. Some of these things we cannot control.

But there are some things we can.

Creating our own culture is something we can do, regardless of what is going on around us.

In the last story, I talked about the overwhelming culture of the membership club and how so much of that culture felt compromising and unsafe. I also mention the culture that I was able to create, within my teams and with the members.

I had control over how I behaved as a boss and a director. I had a position of power and I used it to create my own culture. And that culture felt good. It supported me and other women. And ninety percent of the time, this culture was my reality.

Is there a culture you can create that makes you feel good?

It can be as small as asking a coworker if they would like anything from the bodega on the corner. That simple question can create a culture of kindness and consideration on your floor at work.

It can be asking another mom at pickup how she has been feeling. Asking a question not just about her kids or the school schedule, but about her.

By creating microcultures that align with our value systems, we can exert some control over our reality.

We may not yet be able to fully change some of the larger cultures we inhabit, but what we can do is create cultures that feel right to us, the kind of cultures that honor us and lift us up.

If you have some power, empower someone else.

This Onwards appears with this story because this was the point in my career when I began to have more power, and this Onwards is the single most important thing I can think to do with that power.

Women are so consistently told their greatest assets are the way that they look and their relationship to men, whether as a mother, wife, mistress, etc. While a generalization with, thankfully, more than a few anomalies, it is still one of our more prevailing story lines.

It's time for a new story.

I believe the answer is to empower more women to work for themselves or to gain positions of power within companies, and then for us to create cultures that support and promote women and other minorities.

This is the way we will finally break free from the dominant paradigm.

You do not have to be the founder of your own company or sitting in the executive suite to do this. If you have some power, you can empower someone else. As a woman, you can find another woman who is just starting out in a company you have been at for years. You can give her some advice that will improve her experience, and that will set her up for success.

One of my favorite memories from working at the company that will feature in the next story happened in the employee kitchen one day. I believe it illustrates this Onwards well.

I came into the company as a vice president and was therefore given an office on what was called "the executive floor." I was down the hall and around the corner from the four top men in the company. There were about forty other men on this floor. There were twenty women as well, but only a few of us had executive titles. The rest were assistants. They had desks outside of the executives' closed-door offices.

There was an expansive, open-floor-plan kitchen where people would make sandwiches or heat up leftovers. This kitchen was fully stocked and ten times nicer than the one in my small apartment.

One day, I was rinsing my soup bowl and putting it in the dishwasher when I noticed the sink was full of dirty dishes.

It was a busy day for the company, with clients coming in and out all afternoon.

I started to wash the other dishes and load them into the dishwasher.

A woman named Lily came up next to me and slapped my hand that was holding the sponge.

"Stop it," she said, taking the sponge out of my hand and returning it to its holder.

I was brand new to the company and hadn't gotten to know Lily yet. She had been there for a few years and was a top performer in her department.

Lily looked at me sternly.

"Those are not your dishes. Whoever's they are should put them away. If you do this, even one time, they are going to expect you to do it all the time. This is *not* your job, and don't you dare let them think that it is."

Her point landed hard. Lily was right. I had never thought of it before, but of course a woman, walking into a dirty kitchen, is going to have the instinct to put the dishes away. That is how we have been raised. Did I think most of the men on that floor would have the same thought?

This simple story reveals so much of the conditioning and dynamics that exist around traditional male and female roles. But for me, in that moment, the revelation was instant, and lasting.

Lily empowered me on that day with one simple lesson.

The point is that it can be a small act, but if you have any power, empower someone else.

THE TOP OF THE CORPORATE LADDER, MY PERSONAL LOW

Whenever I tell people about my time as a membership director, one part of the story always fascinates them: I call it the "great purge."

One of my first assignments on the job was to refine the membership. To do this I was asked to cancel the memberships of over four hundred people.

The reasoning is murky. During the economic downturn brought on by the recession, the club needed more revenue, so it let in more members.

When the economy stabilized, the club wanted to go back to being more curated and specialized.

It was my job to remove the members that were no longer wanted.

The entire process took about six months. I often felt like I was the most hated person in all of New York City. I would send an email informing someone that their membership had been canceled. In the email, I would explain that the person was allowed to appeal.

An "appeal" was sitting down in person with me.

Ninety-five percent of these appeals were with men. The meetings would go one of two ways. In one scenario, the man would arrive, upset, before he even sat down. He would open by aggressively asking if I knew how much money he spent at the club (I didn't). Sometimes he would even say, "Do you know who I am?"

(I did. And I didn't care.)

I never renewed any of these men's memberships.

In the other scenario, the man would come in and ask questions. He would try to understand why this was happening.

These men would listen and respond that they understood. They would say they were disappointed but appreciated the chance to meet.

I would renew these memberships.

The renewed members were always grateful. A few of them became my friends. We would joke about how I had "saved" them.

So, it wasn't entirely surprising when, a few years later, one of these men called me out of the blue. I was still working for the membership club company, but in a strategy role that allowed me to work remotely. I had recently moved back to Los Angeles with a new girlfriend.

The man called to see if I could take a meeting with him next week in New York City. He had just started a big new job as chief marketing officer of a multibillion-dollar company.

He said he had a potential job for me.

As fate would have it, I was already scheduled to spend the next week in New York. I agreed to meet with him. I was curious about what he was going to propose.

A week later we met at the membership club to have a drink. The CMO was excited as he shared his news. He had been poached by his CEO to join the new company. Their mission was to "reinvent the brand." He wanted to make a two-hundred-year-old art company "hip and relevant," he said.

He told me he thought I was just the person to do it.

I was flattered but incredulous. What I knew about his new company was that it was worlds away from being hip and relevant. The company existed at the highest end of the "art world." It did hundreds of millions of dollars in sales. The brand name was known for being pretentious and stuffy.

Over our drinks, I expressed doubt that the company would want anything to do with me, a heavily tattooed lesbian.

The CMO was relentless in his pitch. He told me he called the shots now. He said I was *exactly* what the company needed. He asked for the chance to put together an offer that I couldn't refuse.

I didn't have anything to lose at that point, so I agreed.

A week later, I was presented with the offer. I was to come in as a vice president, in charge of two departments. The salary was nearly double what I was making, and there would be an additional signing bonus *and* a relocation fee.

It was a great professional opportunity and a lot of money. I couldn't find a reason to say no.

Instead of flying back to Los Angeles, I stayed in New York City. I went through a grueling two weeks of interviews at the company.

I got the job and everything that the CMO had promised I would get.

I called the owner of the membership club. He was traveling in the United States and agreed to add a short trip to New York City to meet with me.

We sat down for lunch, and I told him about the offer with the art company. He didn't hesitate in telling me I absolutely had to take it. I could tell that he was impressed with the money and position they were offering. The owner of the membership club told me I would always have a place with his company. After that conversation, I was ready to sign.

I shipped my belongings from LA and found an apartment, sight unseen, less than a block away from the company headquarters on the Upper East Side. The apartment was one of those New York City luxury apartments with a concierge desk, an Olympic-size swimming pool, and a fully equipped gym.

In less than a month, I had a completely different life than the one I had been living.

The CMO wanted to make an event of my signing my contract. We agreed to do it on the morning of my birthday, with a September start date a week later.

We planned to meet for breakfast.

When the CMO arrived, he looked disheveled. Before he sat down, he started jabbering that "it is all going to be okay, the contract will go through." He said there had been an "incident."

I was very confused.

The CMO sat down and explained that because he had put me in charge of two departments at the company, it had caused some havoc. The two men who had been running the departments had been told they would be reporting to someone new. The CMO explained that both men were longtime employees. One had been there for eighteen years, and the other for twenty.

They had been given the option of either staying and working under me or taking a voluntary separation package. If they chose the latter, they would receive a severance but be out of a job.

The CMO told me that one of these men had committed suicide the night before.

I was speechless. I hadn't even started my job yet and *this* was the news I was getting?

The CMO assured me that the man's suicide had nothing to do with the news he had received. But I couldn't wrap my brain around how it couldn't have played a part.

My heart broke for someone I never even had the chance to meet.

We still signed the contract. I had already moved my entire life back to New York City for this job. And I had quit my job with the club.

I started work on September 5, as planned.

There are no words to describe what it was like to walk into the headquarters for the first time.

I had back-to-back meetings scheduled with my new teams.

It was immediately clear that I was the enemy.

I had come in with the new regime, and I represented all that was awful about the change.

I could feel that people associated me with what was happening to longtime employees of the company.

I felt the brunt of all this because I worked side by side with other employees. I wasn't safely encased in a big glass office with a door that locked. The CMO that hired me was protected.

If he knew what was happening, (he did), he could easily choose to ignore it. (He did.)

I did not have that luxury.

I did the only thing I knew how to do. I tried to be sensitive and kind. The employees that had worked under the man who had committed suicide were understandably distraught. I listened to their stories about him. I encouraged them to take the time they needed to grieve and heal.

The other man I was meant to replace had been best friends with the man that died. I expressed my sincere condolences. I did my best not to cry in front of him. After all, I didn't know his best friend. I was overwhelmed with emotions—guilt, specifically—for something I had nothing to do with but felt responsible for.

I invited this man to lunch.

It was a truly awful meeting for both of us.

I couldn't get over my sense that I was responsible for everything bad that was happening.

For two decades, this man had worked alongside his best friend, and now his best friend was gone. And I was there to replace them both.

The man I had lunch with was excellent at his job. But because he represented the "old guard," the CEO and CMO saw him as dispensable.

At lunch, I did my best to express my willingness to find a solution that worked for both of us. I offered to let him keep his big office. I told him I would fill one of the empty, open desks. I told him he could continue to oversee his team.

I knew I could learn from him, and I told him so. I said that together we could figure out how to comanage the department and work together.

When word got back to the CEO that I'd had this discussion, the CEO marched into the CMO's office where I was sitting and slammed the door.

He glared at me and shouted, "Do you have 'IDIOT' tattooed on your fucking forehead?"

I was stunned. I had barely spoken with the CEO since being hired. This was one of the first things he said to me. And it was laced with profanity and rage.

The CEO stormed out. I looked at the CMO, my protector in this situation. Or so I thought. He just sat there with his mouth open. The best he could do was to mutter an "I'm sorry." The CMO had put me in this impossible situation, but I realized in that moment that I was going to be alone in figuring it out.

I had just gotten berated by the head of the company for my attempt at resolution.

Soon after, The man I had taken to lunch decided to take the voluntary separation package. He told me the severance package was a good one, and that he could use a break after all that had transpired. He thanked me for trying to find a solution for him, but said he realized his time at the company was done.

I now oversaw two departments with over a dozen people reporting to me. It was evident that in their eyes, I was the reason they lost their beloved bosses.

The CMO set out to make changes, both large and small, to the brand identity of the company. We would meet every morning, before eight, when he would share his goals for the day.

After that morning meeting, it was up to me to make everything happen. I was responsible for actualizing the changes the CMO wanted to see. This was absolutely part of my job; however, it often put me in the crosshairs of others at the company. Because many of the changes involved doing things in a new and different way, the changes disturbed the status quo. Since I was the one implementing the changes, I was the one that was blamed. The CMO never had to face any of the ire from longtime employees. In a cruel manifestation of the phrase "shooting the messenger," I suffered numerous metaphorical bullet holes, every day.

Three months into my time at the art company, I was finding my stride. Although I was often the bearer of bad news (as dictated by the CMO), I felt I was slowly gaining the respect of my colleagues and my direct reports. I would always go the extra mile to find compromises around new systems. No one could deny how hard I worked or the strength of my dedication to my team. I told a friend that the job had been the best diet ever, because in the first three months of work, I had lost twelve pounds. I had so much to do, I never stopped to eat.

One day at a team meeting, the CMO announced he was bringing in a head of partnerships. It was an old friend of his from his media company days.

I will call him "Mike."

Mike came on board as an executive vice president.

I knew that my starting title of vice president was a stretch, but bringing someone in as an EVP felt preposterous.

On the day he started, Mike was given an assistant and a giant glass office on the executive floor. Mike borrowed tens of millions of dollars of art to decorate his new office.

Within one month, it was clear to everyone that Mike was useless at his job.

Worse, he was dismissive and verbally abusive to his assistant.

She would beg me to help her get transferred to my department.

Mike was also an active cocaine user. He was prone to fits of near-hysterical energy. Mike was the messiest person I've ever worked around. He left a path of destruction everywhere he went.

The CMO staunchly defended him on countless occasions. He stood up for Mike to the CEO, the CFO, and in front of the board. It was only after Mike single-handedly lost the biggest media account the company had, that the CMO knew he had to fire him.

There is no doubt Mike walked away with a handsome settlement. The CMO protected him from day one and continued to protect him when he was let go.

After Mike was gone, the CMO found me at my desk and told me I was to take over Mike's department. I would now be running three departments for the company.

There was no salary increase and no office. The CMO was having me clean up the mess that Mike had made.

In my second year at the company, I was promoted to senior vice president. I was proud of the promotion, and I recognized I was being acknowledged for my hard work.

As was true in the last story, most of the work situations I found myself in were not all good or all bad. With this promotion came the most recognition I had received. And it looked like it this trend of success was going to continue.

One morning, the CMO called me into his office to tell me that the *New York Times* was going to run a story on the company. The *Times* wanted to write a feature on all the innovation our group had accomplished. He told me to be on the lookout for a call. I was excited to be interviewed for the article. The call never came.

An article did come out in the *New York Times*. It was a full two pages, filled with quotes from the CMO. He took credit for every program that I had started with my team. The article highlighted the interesting partners from outside the art world that the CMO had brought in to work with. The truth was that I had introduced him to every one of those future partners. They were a part of my personal network.

In private, the CMO always thanked me profusely. He was constantly telling me how he "couldn't do it without me," and how I "single-handedly made everything work."

In addition to our daily in-person meetings at eight, the CMO used to call me on his way to the gym in the morning. The call would come in somewhere between 6:00 a.m. and 7:30. I had to plan my workouts and getting ready for work around these calls. The purpose of the call was always for the CMO to offload his stress and anxiety about the day ahead.

In addition to being his most trusted employee, I felt I was fulfilling the role of his therapist, and of his work spouse. Every day I felt like I had to be both things.

The CMO was a dramatic guy. He never held back his emotions with me, whether personal or professional. There were a few times when the CMO expressed so much emotion, I thought he would cry.

One of these times involved a newly appointed member to the company's board of directors. This member was a close friend of the CMO's from his media days. The first time I met this board member, I instantly got a bad vibe. I could tell he was a lascivious guy and that I had sparked his interest.

The board member asked me to have a meal with him. When I told the CMO, he seemed excited that this board member was taking such an interest in our projects. I asked the CMO if he really believed that was the motive for the invite. The CMO told me the board member was going through a divorce but still totally in love with his wife, and that he was totally harmless.

I accepted the dinner invitation, against my better judgment, because I believed there was a chance the board member had asked me to dinner to hear my ideas for growth for the company.

During dinner, it became apparent that he was interested in me romantically.

I felt like kicking myself. I had known this was his motivation, but I let myself be convinced otherwise.

I told the board member that I was a gay woman and was not interested in any sort of relationship with him outside of a professional one.

In our meeting the next day, I told the CMO what had happened. He laughed it off and told me I had a charm that went beyond sexuality.

That wasn't helpful.

For the next six months, I had to navigate the situation with this board member. Most of the time he would be polite, but still a little overattentive to me compared to other people in the office. Shortly after he moved to Los Angeles, I had to travel there to host an event. The environment at the event was decidedly more social. The board member, despite knowing of my sexuality and lack of interest, made an egregious pass at me. I had to push him off and ended up leaving a day early just to avoid seeing him at another event the next day.

I called the CMO the moment I landed back in New York. He expressed shock and said he was horrified for me. And then he said that it didn't surprise him. He told me that he knew the board member had issues. The CMO apologized profusely and made such a display of emotions—outrage, indignance, anger, compassion—that I believed the situation would be handled.

And then, nothing happened.

The board member remained on the board. The CMO would pal around with him during meetings. I avoided the board member for the rest of my time at the company, and as much as I was grateful to the CMO for giving me the opportunity, I was beginning to understand that he was never going to stick his neck out for me. He was never going to stand up for me or make sure I was safe.

And as for the board member, the situation served as an awful and sobering reminder to me that powerful men can do horrible things, and nothing will happen to them.

A few months passed and I was asked to go to Arizona for an event with one of our affiliate companies. The deal between my company and the man that owned the affiliate was an important one. It represented hundreds of millions of dollars of yearly revenue.

I was told it was essential that we had a happy working relationship with this man. When this company owner came to New York to meet the team, the CMO introduced me as his "star player."

The owner instantly took a liking to me. He was flirty and kept finding ways to touch me. On the arm, or the shoulder—it was almost constant. Again, I felt unsafe where I worked. But because this man's company was based overseas, I didn't think I would be spending any time with him.

Until Arizona.

I was surprised I was being asked to attend these events. The affiliate company wasn't part of one of my three departments. The CMO told me that the owner of the company had specifically asked that I attend.

I felt uneasy the whole plane ride. Because the affiliate company wasn't under my jurisdiction, I didn't have any work to do in Arizona. I had no idea what I was supposed to do for two days in the middle of the desert. I had no business or purpose for being there.

My CMO and the CEO were staying at the Ritz-Carlton in Phoenix. The rest of our company's employees were staying at a hotel a few miles away.

I was surprised when I saw on my itinerary that I had been booked at the Ritz-Carlton.

When we arrived at the hotel, I went to the desk to check in. The man behind the desk welcomed me as "Mrs. X," the last name of the owner of the affiliate company.

He had booked me in his hotel suite.

I got a pit in my stomach. I asked but was told there were no other rooms available. The man at the desk explained that it was their largest suite on the property. He said it was essentially two individual suites separated by a door.

I went to the room and discovered there was no lock on the adjoining door.

On the dining room table were flowers and a note from the owner of the affiliate company. He asked if I would join him for dinner that evening.

I wrote a note back to the man and told him I would not be joining him for dinner.

I wrote that I was entirely uncomfortable with the room situation.

I said that I felt compromised and unsafe.

I spoke up. A little bit.

I slipped the note under the door to his room and moved the couch in front of the door to act as a lock.

When we saw each other later that evening, he apologized to me. He said he thought the adjoining suites would be "fun." He said he imagined we could have breakfasts together.

He continued to make advances on me, all three days we were in Phoenix, but he knew better than to come into my room.

I told the CMO about all this while we were still in Phoenix. It was early one morning, and we were on a walk. The CMO acted the same way he had when I told him about the board member. He expressed disgust and horror. He said he couldn't believe the audacity the man had to think he could do that to me. The CMO teared up. He said that he understood how unfair the world was to women. He had a twenty-one-year-old daughter, and he said that hearing what happened to me made him worry for her.

I believed the CMO would help me this time. I thought he would say or do something, anything.

He did nothing.

The last straw came during a huge blow up with the CEO. It happened at about 7:45 p.m. one evening. I was still working but trying to wrap things up and go home.

The CMO had left for the night. I was finishing some important work with one of my assistants. She was overseeing one of our larger events of the year. It was a charity event for one of our biggest clients. My company had hosted this event for over a decade. Every year it was pretty much the same. This year, the charity director had called my assistant and said that this year the foundation wanted to change things up.

The charity director requested a female speaker for the event this year. For the last decade, the same man had given the keynote. There was a woman in the company that the charity director had come to know, and she was who they specifically requested to host the evening.

Since the request was coming from the charity itself, my assistant agreed to make the change.

What I didn't know was that when the male keynote speaker who had been replaced found out, he called the CEO to complain.

Now, my name was being shouted down the hall of the executive suite floor. It was the CEO, and he was screaming for me. I went over to his office and found him standing outside the glass doors, his face purple with rage.

He let loose a string of expletives. One stood out. "Fucking feminist dyke!" he seethed while pointing at me.

There were a few other people still at their desks. I don't think anyone took a breath.

The CEO moved closer until he was inches from my face. I flashed back to all these tiny moments of violence I had seen from him. The way the CEO would grab his wife by the upper arm when she had too much wine at an event. I could see his grip tighten until her skin turned red.

I backed away and looked toward the CMO's office, which was dark. I realized the CEO was under the impression that I had made the program change on my own. He thought I had replaced the male speaker with a female. He was raving that I had a "feminist agenda" because I was a "fucking dyke."

I tried to explain how the charity director had reached out to my assistant and requested the change. At this point, the CEO shifted his attention to my assistant. He shouted at the nearest terrified onlooker to go get her.

I looked down the hallway and saw that my assistant was already walking toward us. I sprang into action. I turned away from the CEO and rushed towards my assistant. I put my hands on her shoulders and turned her in the other direction. I told her to get her things and go home immediately. There was no way I was going to subject this woman to the CEO.

While he was still shouting at us, I kept walking down the hallway. I walked right into the HR office. To my surprise there was a woman still at her desk. I informed her I was resigning, effective immediately. Then I left the building.

I walked the half a block to my apartment and poured myself a very large glass of wine.

About forty-five minutes later, my cell phone rang.

It was the CEO. I didn't answer. He called back a few more times.

Fifteen minutes later, the front desk attendant of my apartment building called to tell me I had a visitor. They put him on the phone. It was the CEO. He had walked over to my apartment building and was standing in the lobby.

The CEO apologized. He told me he had found out what happened and realized he had made a mistake. He said he had been informed that I had resigned and asked if I would reconsider.

I didn't hesitate for one moment to give my answer.

No, I said. I would not reconsider.

The next day, the CMO was devastated. It was the third time I saw him tear up over something that happened to me.

He called me into his office and went on and on about how he should have been there for me. He said he should have protected me. He promised he would speak up about the CEO. He said he would defend me. He promised he would take care of me.

As it turned out, the CMO said nothing.

He did not go on record defending me. I was offered a moderate settlement, on condition that I say that I was fired, not that I quit, and provided I sign an NDA. I considered suing but couldn't imagine spending the next two years in litigation.

I just wanted out.

The company sold a year after I left. The CEO and CMO walked away with millions.

The CMO still calls me, mostly to ask for advice about his daughter, who recently came out as gay. He asks me how to handle certain situations, or he asks me to help her with her career. From time to time, he asks me to review a potential investment he is considering. I always end up helping him. Which pisses me off.

The CMO probably has no idea of how I really feel. I have carried an anger with me since I left the art company in 2017.

When I made the choice to resign and take the small settlement, I didn't have enough money to take my time finding my next thing. I had to hustle to reinvent myself, yet again. Conversely, the CMO left with such a large severance that he retired. He started traveling the world and posting Instagram stories about his trips.

Seeing one of these posts would make my blood boil. But I said nothing.

When I was raising funds for my start-up, the CMO promised to support me. He said he was traveling but that as soon as he got back to the United States, he would make an investment.

I followed up three times. I never heard back.

Dear CMO,

I believe on some level you knew that this was coming. How could you not? You shed tears in front of me knowing the times you utterly failed me.
I am finally brave enough to say something.
We had both a professional and personal relationship. I believe I know you well as a man, and as a father. I know how much your daughter means to you.
She called me before she came out as gay to you. She wanted to make sure I would be there for you to talk through things if you needed it.
I told her I would be. And I was.
It is just another time that I was there for you. That I helped you.
What is so damn interesting about this is that even though you have so much more influence, and money, and power than I do, it was always me, helping you.
A part of that is on me. I have a hard time saying no when someone asks me for something. I'm working on that. This letter isn't about that.
This letter is about what I need to tell you.
Something I believe in my heart you already know.
You are a coward.
You never stood up for me because you were afraid of what it might jeopardize for you.
Even when you knew things were wrong, and that I was being hurt, you were afraid to speak up. You sacrificed my safety because you were afraid of what it might cost you.
Do you have any idea how devastating this was for me to see, and to feel?
I trusted you. I believed in you. And in a few awful situations, I needed you.
And you weren't there.

I thought that coming to you was my way of speaking the fuck up.
You were my superior and the only person I reported to, so I believed telling you what was happening was my way of reporting it and that you would be obligated to do something.
You did nothing.
What you did to me by staying silent was far worse than what was done to me.
You knew what happened. It was bad enough to make you cry.
But you couldn't risk your own livelihood to speak up for my personhood.
This makes you a coward.
If you had said something, I know it would have given me the courage to say something too. I would have felt that I had an ally, a support, a friend.
You couldn't do this for me. And now I must do it for myself.
I'm starting with you.
You failed me. And I know that deep down, you know you failed yourself too. You are not the man you want to be. You are not brave, or bold, or an ally to women.
You are not the evolved, sensitive, anomalous man you imagine yourself to be.
You can't speak up when you see something wrong. Not when it might cost you a bit of your comfort or security.
Because of this, I can't respect you.
I have such a long way to go on my journey of speaking the fuck up.
But you haven't even started.
You had the chance to be so much better. You could have made such a difference and affected real change at the company you were hired to change.
But you didn't. You stayed silent, and this makes you complicit in everything I went through.
This makes you a perpetrator and not an ally.
You are currently traveling the world, climbing mountains,

searching for enlightenment.
Instead, why don't you start here?
Rachel

HINDSIGHTS

As I relived the experience at this company through this story and letter, I realized that I never even thought to write a letter to the CEO.

Even though he was the one that felt physically threatening, and the one that called me a "Fucking Dyke" and an "Idiot," I never thought about writing to him. I never even think about him.

Instead, all my energy and memories involve how disappointing it was to believe I had an ally in the CMO—my boss, but also my friend. The father of a gay daughter. I truly believed this man was on my side and that he would help me. Beyond our personal connection, I was an excellent employee. I answered the phone every morning when he called before seven a.m. to share his anxieties about the day. I worked as late as was needed to create and complete what he wanted.

My first hindsight is questioning why I was so sure that this man was my ally.

Maybe it was because he talked a great game, always going on about equity and diversity in the workplace, but in truth, all he really cared about was money.

It was never about the money for me, but in hindsight, I see it was always and only about the financial and job security for him. That was his motivation, and I now see that it was also all he truly cared about.

Now, I look back and wonder why I felt it was so necessary to do so much, to always go above and beyond. And I wonder, just like I did when telling the previous story, why I didn't set *any* boundaries to honor my personal space or my personal time, or to protect my emotional and mental well-being.

There is so much to unpack here about the inequities between men and women in the workplace, it would take another three books.

Besides the wild economic disparity, there is another dynamic that exists when women work for men. Put simply, we "cash the checks their mouths write." I love this expression because it is so completely true.

This CMO would have an idea, or he would want to try something new, so he would say it to me. And then I had to go make it happen while he did nothing.

I had to cash the checks his mouth wrote.

Again, not having another three books yet to break this all down, I will simply say this.

Women work harder than men and they work better than men.

That is a bold and brazen hindsight, but I stand by it one hundred percent.

This is the company where Lily told me not to do the dishes. The culture was so egregiously sexist that I would bet my last dollar that all the dirty dishes in that sink were left by men, thinking that some woman would take care of it.

Despite the sexist culture at the company, there were times when I imagine the long and lucrative career I could have had if I had stayed. There were things I loved about the work, and I know I was an excellent boss to the young women and men that reported to me. I was in a position of power, and I worked hard to create a culture of kindness and collaboration within the larger company culture. Within my smaller units, every voice was heard.

My final hindsight from this story is that this was the experience that solidified a feeling that was growing in me.

I didn't want to work for men anymore.

I would work for myself, or I would work for a woman, but I no longer believed in men enough to work for them.

At this point in my career, I wasn't there yet. I had to go through a lot more before I would finally get there, but this is the experience that really set this determination in me.

I wanted to write and cash my own checks, not the ones *his* mouth wrote.

ONWARDS

Find an ally. Check your allies.

In work and in life, it is so important to have allies. This Onwards is about considering who you believe could be an ally, but also about running a bit of a background check on the allies that you do have.

At this company, I thought that a powerful man, the man who hired me and brought me in, would act as an ally for me. I wasn't wrong to assume that. He could have, and he should have, but he didn't. He was a coward. Furthermore, in a patriarchal society, there are rarely any consequences for *not* speaking up for women.

Is there anyone you assume would be there for you if you needed them? Can you have a conversation in the hypothetical, to check?

This Onwards requires you to listen to your gut. Think about the people you believe are your allies and see how you feel about them when you close your eyes. Have they already been there for you in the past? Do you believe they would be there for you, no questions asked, if something happened? Those are your allies.

Look for the groups of women.

This Onwards makes me smile as I type it.

Close your eyes and imagine coming upon a group of four or six or ten women, gathered together and talking excitedly. Undoubtedly, there will be something fun or important in the works.

Is there a group of women that you know of doing things that matter to you? If not, can you make one? If this isn't possible or feasible because of where you live or your life circumstances, is there a group you can follow online?

Writing this book often made me think about the #MeToo movement, for obvious reasons. While the organized movement itself may have been the target of some valid criticism, there was undeniable value in how #MeToo gave women a platform to speak up. Even if it was just with a hashtag.

Most of the voices speaking the fuck up were women, and when counted together, there was social and economic weight to this collective.

Having that weight feels good. It feels like one giant ally, letting you know you are not alone and that there are other women going through what you are going through.

I wholeheartedly believe in the power of community. I've built a career on it.

For this Onwards, see what communities are available to you.

The wonderful news is that If you are reading this book, you are in the Speak the Fuck Up community. There is a place for you here.

You belong here.

HOLLYWOOD PART TWO—ALL THAT GLITTERS IS NOT GOLD

After almost three years in New York City, I was ready for a change. I did the thing that was now most familiar to me. I traded one coast for the other. I moved back to Los Angeles. I had no problem getting out of my lease in New York City, but I wasn't ready to sign another in Los Angeles.

When I first got back to the West Coast, I was again licking my wounds. I needed something to inspire me and cheer me up.

I decided to be impulsive and check myself into my favorite hotel in LA: the Chateau Marmont.

I had stayed there many times over the last decade. For me, the hotel represented decadence, but also a sort of "falling off the radar" possibility. I wasn't ready to work again. I wasn't ready to be fully in the world again. Checking in to the hotel allowed me to remain removed from the real world while I healed.

When the hotel asked, I informed them it was for a "long-term" stay. I signed a contract for two months with the ability to extend. I was literally spending my entire settlement on the hotel. I didn't care.

In retrospect, I think I was having a midlife crisis.

I had such high hopes for my extended stay at the Chateau. I imagined I would finally become a writer. It was all I wanted to be since I was a child sitting alone in my room, plumbing the depths of my heart and the inescapable loneliness that comes with being human. If this sounds dramatic, don't forget that in this scenario I am also listening to Linda Ronstadt sing about settling for *any* warm body in the lonely night.

I imagined I would wake up with the sun to write at my little wooden desk. I would write all morning long and then go for a swim and have a light lunch before returning to my room. I would write again until about three in the afternoon, when I would take a stroll through the Chateau garden. I would make my way to the hotel bar and sip on a scotch while I contemplated my plans for the evening. I would have a fabulous dinner, fabulous wine, and do the whole thing over again the next day.

What happened was the exact opposite. I woke up later and later every day. My first thought was always how much money I was spending.

I would make instant coffee and stare at a blank page on my computer until about eleven in the morning.

I would walk to Trader Joe's for groceries. I would walk the Hollywood hills for exercise. Every night I would make dinner in my room, usually pasta and canned tomato sauce. I would drink five-dollar bottles of wine and fall asleep watching *Access Hollywood* at a ridiculously early hour.

My midlife crisis cost me over $20,000 in hotel bills. Despite this astronomical amount, I was most likely the Chateau Marmont's least favorite long-term guest. I didn't spend a cent outside of what the room cost. No minibar, no room service or eating in the restaurant. I was the most frugal luxury hotel guest there ever was.

I ended up hating my two months at the Chateau. Instead of setting me free, it locked me in a mildly depressive, reclusive state of being. I thought living out this fantasy would make me happy, and instead it made me a little insane and a lot broke. It was time to go back to work.

One of my former colleagues had recently invested in a new venture in Los Angeles. She called and told me she thought it was right up my alley. It was going to be a fancy private members club. It would cater exclusively to the "Hollywood A-list" crowd.

She said the owner was looking for someone to help him get it off the ground and she thought of me.

I agreed to meet with the Club Owner in an exploratory capacity. We met at one of the other properties he owned. The meeting could not have gone better. He was nothing short of fawning—over my experience, my style, my connections, all of it.

He also had to be aware that the young woman who connected us was the heir to a massive family fortune. She had influence on account of her legacy. And she was young and beautiful and represented the "new guard" for Hollywood.

After a couple of weeks, we hammered out an agreement to work together. The Club Owner continuously expressed his need for our partnership. He was an excellent hotelier and businessman, but had no experience with membership. We would be a team of two.

The Club Owner didn't sign the contract I presented to protect myself as an independent consultant. He said that if I wanted to go down the route of legal paperwork, he would engage his team of lawyers. He said it would take months. I wasn't comfortable with his dismissal of my need to secure my position, but I went forward anyway. He also asked me to work with him exclusively. He didn't want word getting around town that I was a "consultant for hire." He demanded loyalty.

I agreed, but still felt unsettled. The Club Owner negotiated me down on my price too. But he remained adamant about our partnership. He told me that this was going to be the beginning of many great things. And he was incessantly fawning.

We shook hands and began our work together.

Things started out well. A few months in, we started to build a team. I suggested that the Club Owner have everyone sign an NDA. The staff would be privy to information about some of the biggest celebrities in the world.

The Club Owner told me I was being paranoid. Still, he must have gone home and talked to his spouse, or a trusted friend. The next day, he came into the office and told me he had decided that we needed an NDA. He asked if I had completed it yet. I shared what I had written with him. We made copies and had everyone sign.

After a small staff was put in place, things took a turn for the worse.

I was the only person that the Club Owner communicated with every day. The project was an intensely personal one for him. I started to use the metaphor with friends that I felt like he was running for prom king in high school, and I was put in charge of his campaign.

In the early months, many of my interactions were with the Club Owner's investors. To get the project off the ground, he had taken on nearly fifty investors, and they all wanted updates and favors. The Club Owner sent them all to me.

Eventually, he would end up consolidating with one major investor and paying back his initial investors at a small profit. For many investors, this felt like a slap in the face. Again, I was their point of contact, and I had to handle the fallout.

One morning, the Club Owner called me just after six in the morning, as he typically did. He sounded frenetic on the phone. He asked me if I knew anyone who could get four front-row seats and backstage passes to see Taylor Swift. He told me he needed the tickets for that coming Friday night's show. It was Tuesday. And it was Taylor Swift.

I panicked. I had no idea if I knew anyone that could do that.

I asked the Club Owner why it was so important.

He turned curt. "They are for a very important investor. *Very* important. The opening of this club depends on it."

This felt serious. I hung up and wracked my brain.

I had one friend in LA in the music business. His name was Nick.

I actually didn't know Nick all that well, but he had made an incredible first impression on me. When I was working for the art company, someone had introduced me to Nick, who helped with curating some musicians for an event. Nick went above and beyond, and he made me look great in front of the CEO and CMO. When Nick moved from New York to Los Angeles with his wife Christina, we stayed in intermittent contact.

In desperation, I called Nick.

"Whew," he said. "That's a tough one. And Taylor doesn't officially do any meet and greets anymore." He paused while I sweated on the other end of the line.

Then Nick asked, "Is this *really* important to you?"

"Yes, Nick. Yes it is. I think my job might depend on it."

"OK, let me see what I can do."

No more than an hour later, Nick called me with the news. He had talked to Taylor's label and secured four front-row tickets and backstage passes. I gave him the name and address of the investor and thanked him profusely.

I asked what it would cost.

"I called in a favor," Nick said. "A big one. No charge."

I was elated, and frankly, quite proud of myself for accomplishing this almost impossible task.

I called the Club Owner and told him the news. He didn't acknowledge just what an incredible feat this was, he just asked how I did it.

"I called my friend Nick. He's the best! I would love to offer him a membership! He's not charging us anything."

The Club Owner was barely listening. "When will the tickets get there?" he asked.

I told the Club Owner that FedEx would be two-day delivery for arrival on Thursday.

And then I went about my day.

Thursday came, and at about four in the afternoon, the Club Owner called me and started screaming. "There are no fucking tickets, Rachel!"

I started to panic again. That couldn't be possible.

I called Nick who immediately got on with the label, which confirmed the tickets had indeed gone out. They gave Nick the FedEx tracking number.

I may have been crying at this point, so Nick volunteered to connect with FedEx for me.

An hour and three phone calls from the Club Owner later, Nick called me.

"FedEx lost the package."

I felt like I was going to faint. How could this possibly happen?

I called the Club Owner, who immediately went ballistic.

"I *knew* it!" he shrieked. "We've been conned! Your guy Nick is totally conning us! It's a scam! You set us up for a scam!"

I was shocked. How could *free* tickets (Nick wasn't even charging us for FedEx!) be a scam? What did anyone possibly have to gain from this gratuitous transaction?

I tried to remind the Club Owner of this fact, but he was having none of it. When he started calling Nick every derogatory name in the book, I hung up.

Nick called me back.

"I talked to the label. They never do this, but they are going to reissue the tickets. I will pay to have them messengered over to the guy's house first thing in the morning."

And he did.

Four front-row seats and backstage passes to a Taylor Swift concert *for free*, for a man whose name I never even knew except to get his address.

When I told the Club Owner that the tickets had been hand delivered, and signed for, at the front door of the investor's house, instead of saying thank you, he said something about how close we were cutting the whole thing.

The Club Owner barely even said 'thank you' to me, and he never acknowledged Nick or what he had done for us. The moment he heard the tickets had made it to the investor, the Club Owner started in on other things for me to do.

I took Nick and Christina to dinner as a thank-you. I wish I could have done so much more.

Nick, to his incredible credit, shrugged it all off. He told me we were friends and that was just what friends do. Once again, he had gone above and beyond.

If I had to do it all over again, I never would have even asked. Not only did Nick perform a miracle, but he probably saved the Club Owner about $20,000.

The fact that the Club Owner never even asked about Nick, or how he could say thank you, was one of my first signs that the bloom was coming off the rose.

When we opened invitations to join the club to a *very* small group of A-list celebrities, the Club Owner's anxiety skyrocketed. I found myself in the familiar position of needing to constantly assuage his worry and doubt.

As the opening of the club got closer, the Club Owner would often email me before five in the morning. If I didn't respond within minutes, he would call me. He never registered the time of day. The calls would be a torrent of his fears, doubt, and anxiety.

The emails and calls never started with a "Good morning" or a "How are you?" And never once an "I'm sorry to call so early." It was as if my time didn't matter. I was a repository for stress, and nothing more.

I was there to solve any problem, and worse, to do the dirty work of handling any fallout. For every person the Club Owner wanted to be a member, there were ten people that he didn't want to be members.

To their faces, the Club Owner would express enthusiasm and excitement about their interest in the club. He would tell them to reach out to me. And then he would tell me that they would never in a million years receive an invitation to join. Every day leading up to the opening of the club, I had to deal with that.

The Club Owner remained pristine, perfect, and beloved. The only person people blamed when someone didn't get an invitation was me.

I started to make more mistakes, I am embarrassed to say, but I was losing focus. I spent all day dealing with wildly inflated egos, and bruised ones. I was always the bad guy. I was yelled at and threatened, all because I was fulfilling the Club Owner's wishes.

If a big celebrity chose not to join, it immediately became my fault. In the Club Owner's mind, I had done something wrong. The people that the Club Owner had feigned excitement about to their faces would call me, screaming about why they didn't get an invitation to join. Everything had become my fault.

The worst part was when I had to navigate around the subtle, but despicable, racism and sexism from the Club Owner. There were some ethnic groups he did not want to have as members (or employees). He would call them "Canadians." The Club Owner wanted to make sure I didn't hire, or accept, "Canadians" in the club.

I was constantly upset, triggered, and traumatized in the weeks leading up to the club's opening. I stopped being as organized as I always am. The Club Owner harshly berated me for every tiny mistake I would make.

Just before we opened, two of our founding members were publicly accused of sexual assault. One was an A-list celebrity and the other was the head of a huge media empire. I was sure that we would cancel their memberships immediately. Instead, the Club Owner opined about the women that had made the accusations. They were gold diggers, or mentally unstable. He called the female accusers "crazy" and refused to have any more conversations about it with me. Nothing happened with the accused men's memberships.

I knew I had to quit. I gave the Club Owner ninety days' notice.

I had worked so hard to get the club ready to open, I needed to see it through. The moment I stopped being the subservient, loyal employee, I was invisible to the Club Owner.

Three days after I gave notice, he brought in my replacement.

I had to train her and turn everything over to her.

After working tirelessly for over a year, as was his pattern, the Club Owner never even said "thank you."

Dear Club Owner,

You should probably sit down for this.

For someone that hates confrontation, this is going to be a doozy for you.

I have watched you for a year and a half, putting on a show for everyone you run into. You tell them how great they look, how happy you are to see them, only to skewer them moments later behind their back.

Your sexism and racism are so thinly veiled. Your judgment of people that aren't rich and beautiful is shocking. And when it came to me, a woman working for you, your misogyny was blatant.
In the beginning, you pretended to love me, but you despised me. And when I started to see through you and threaten your facade, you had to get rid of me.
Do you remember when I called a meeting with you to tell you that every single one of your employees was miserable and many had come to me about quitting?
Instead of asking for any information, you told me they could all go fuck themselves, that there were plenty of people that would take their jobs.
You are so far away from any self-reflection, it's actually impressive.
The good news for you is that your entire existence is in Hollywood. The place that thrives on people being shells of things with no real emotion or feeling or empathy.
Still, you took it to a whole other level.
You made me your pawn. You used me to make sure you always looked good.
You put me between yourself and your bad behavior. You asked me to cover or ignore your racism and sexism until it was finally too much, and I had to leave.
I had to walk away from a job I could have loved, from a career I could have crushed, because I could no longer ignore who you truly are.
The fact that your club is now a huge success is no surprise to me.
You are excellent at what you do.
But you are not excellent.
Not at all.
Your shiny, successful club has an underbelly of exclusion of the worst kind. And it gives refuge to other horrible men.
I heard you are expanding your empire and opening two new clubs. Your success may very well continue and even increase.
But I believe your true nature will come out. It must.

There is only so long you can keep fooling everyone.
It will just take one woman, or one other person whose well-being and personhood you destroy, to speak up.
You deserve to be taken down.
I could have done it. And I didn't.
And I know you know that.
Rachel

P.S- Remember that fucking Taylor Swift ticket debacle? I do.
You owe Nick a thank you, and an apology and about twenty thousand dollars, given what Taylor Swift tickets go for these days.

HINDSIGHTS

This story is the one that brought me to my breaking point. After my experience with the Club Owner, I made the promise to myself, again, to do everything I could to never work for a man, again.

There are many hindsights I take from this story. The most obvious of which is how a gorgeous surface belied a truly dark and ugly underbelly. And I needed to look beyond the surface.

The private club, which I played the largest role in opening successfully, was exclusive and glamorous and shiny. Behind the scenes, things were entirely different. The culture of what it was to work there was abusive and demeaning.

I should have refused to take the job without a legally binding contract. When the owner scoffed at this, I should have walked away. My financial insecurities didn't afford me the freedom to say no. Or so I told myself.

In hindsight, I should have kept looking, taken other interviews, demanded better.

The Club Owner was racist and sexist. I heard and saw abhorrent things. I would always tell him how he couldn't say or do things, but it wasn't enough. I should have quit months before I did. I should have had more conviction in my own values.

My hope is that through writing this book and leading the Speak the F*ck Up movement, I will never put myself in the position to be so morally compromised again.

I now understand that no paycheck or perceived status is worth what I would lose.

When he was trying to persuade me to take the job, the Club Owner told me that if I worked for him and opened what was destined to be one of the most exclusive clubs in the United States, I would be able to get any job I wanted.

It was true. When people found out that I worked on this club, doors flew open. I had my pick of consulting for the top membership clubs in the world.

Everyone, it seems, is enchanted by the shine of Hollywood.

But what is shiny is not always valuable. This experience cost me in self-respect, so much more than what I gained from it.

I learned, from my time with the Director, and again with the Club Owner, when it comes to Hollywood, and people, all that glitters is not always gold.

ONWARDS

Recognize abuse. Call it by its name.

The Club Owner was verbally and psychologically abusive to me. Even though I started going to therapy again when I started working for him, I didn't always use those words.

This Onwards is essential to learning how to speak the fuck up. We must start using the words that are the hardest to say. We must recognize when someone's behavior is abusive.

I had all the evidence in front of me. The initial fawning and love bombing all served to make me feel safe and appreciated, only to later lead to me being belittled, bullied, and abused.

Women, as part of our nature, usually see the best in people. We give second, third, and fourth chances, and we make excuses for atrocious behavior.

We must stop doing this.

I know firsthand how hard it is to admit that we are in an abusive situation, but we must start doing this. We have to say it first to ourselves. It is the first step to getting help and getting strong.

This is a quiet Onwards, but one of the most powerful ones.

Telling the truth, using the most accurate words, even just to yourself, is the start of speaking the fuck up.

Use the power of "anonymous".

This one sounds like an odd Onwards but let me explain. Don't *be* anonymous. Rather, if you see or experience something, and you need to speak up but are too afraid to, you can do so anonymously.

One of my favorite stories from just after this private club opened is about someone writing the Club Owner an anonymous letter.

The basis for this letter was the attire the Club Owner had selected for his female servers. Imagine a very short skirt, a ruffled top, and a little apron. It was something right out of a plantation in the South, and people noticed. And they talked about it.

The men had sharp blazers with the club emblem on the lapel, while the women donned outfits that made them look like servants.

I immediately brought this up to the Club Owner, who told me I was being ridiculous. He said they were based on an Italian design he saw. Bullshit.

One night, a woman (I know who it was) sent an anonymous note about how offensive the uniforms were.

I'm not sure if it was the note alone, but the uniforms were changed.

In this book, I can't always name names because I know these men are nasty and vindictive and they would come after me. But I am saying *something,* and I know the result will benefit me, and if they read this, hopefully it will benefit them as well.

You may be in a situation where it is too risky to say something. Can you say it anonymously?

Can you get the message out there while keeping yourself safe?

The single greatest thing I have learned in this journey is that just saying it counts too.

It does something. It starts to heal you.

Say something. If you must do it anonymously, so be it.

"Just Walk Away Renee."

Or Megan, or Lydia, or Beth. Whatever your name is.

I love this song and I love this Onwards.

There are some situations, and some people, that are best to just walk clear away from and not look back. Many women have been taught that it is their role to fix things or make things right.

I think it is important to realize when you just can't.

Consider it a form of self-preservation.

If someone shows you who they are, and you just don't like what you see, you should walk away.

Earlier hindsights and onwards address trusting our instincts and seeing things for what they are. If you are in a situation where you intuitively know, "This is not a place I will be respected, or safe, or heard," it's time to double down on those feelings and get the fuck out.

When I wanted to interview a Persian woman to be my assistant and the Club Owner told me that there would never be "Canadians" working for him, I should have found the door.

When he told me that the accused studio head was a "great guy" and that the women accusing him were all mentally unstable, I should have resigned that very moment.

If something happens that goes against *every single fiber* of what you believe in—walk away.

Nothing is worth compromising your values, or your worth.

A PANDEMIC AND A MOUNTAIN VIEW

Once the club in Los Angeles was open, I struggled to find a reason to stay there. I had recently moved into a beautiful home in Silver Lake, but I was lost, and lonely. A string of relationships that ended as quickly as they began didn't help. I loved where I lived, but without a sense of purpose, I felt numb.

I had hit the two-year mark. It was time to go back to New York City.

I arrived in the early summer when the weather was getting warm. Feeling the way I did when I had moved back to LA, I wasn't ready to sign a lease and commit for at least a year. I felt depleted from work and life and needed comfort. Two of my closest friends offered for me to stay with them. I bounced back and forth between the two of them for most of the summer, careful not to wear out my welcome.

During this time, I launched my own consulting company, and I was taking meetings with new clients. The LA Club Owner had asked me to work exclusively for him, but now I was free. I signed five clients to my company by October.

I was finally working for myself and making enough money to live where I wanted to in the city. I found a loft in Soho and moved in with nothing more than my two suitcases. I got a Citi Bike membership and spent the fall and winter biking to clients from Chinatown to Flatiron and everywhere in between. I had purpose and agency over my environment. Most importantly, my values weren't being compromised.

I was happy.

And that's when the pandemic hit.

Along with the rest of the world, the bottom fell out for me. I felt despondent. My dreams were shattered.

Almost overnight, my clients started folding their projects. The effects of Covid in New York City, and where I was in Soho specifically, were harrowing. By the end of March 2020, every store on my street was boarded up. When I walked to get coffee, I would often be one of only two or three people on the streets. To see what was once a bustling neighborhood go totally dark was more than alarming. It was terrifying.

There were also the Black Lives Matter riots. I would watch the chaos from my window at night, fires breaking out steps from my building door.

I called my mom and told her I was coming home.

Back on Cape Cod, I waited to see what would happen. It felt like everything was at a standstill. Four of my five clients completely stopped construction. The fifth client, a club and hotel in Denver, was deciding what they were going to do.

When I got the call from the ownership team that they were going to continue with the build, I was thrilled. I would have something to work on during the pandemic and I would still have money coming in. I devoted all my time to the project.

The Denver Developer asked me to put a team in place. They would work remotely until it was safe to relocate them to Denver. I hired a core team. When it came time to hire the membership director, I did extensive interviewing and cast a wide net.

In my experience, a membership director is the hardest position to fill. Rarely do any prospects have direct membership experience. When I got my first job in membership, I had never even been to a private club. Not only does the ideal person have to be personable and persuasive, but they must also be levelheaded, organized, efficient, and a great team leader.

I narrowed a field of over forty people down to three. One man and two women. The man had significant hospitality experience as a restaurant general manager. I was confident he could adapt to the added focus of membership. The first woman came from the corporate world and had spent her career working for luxury brands. Although she didn't have much hospitality experience, she was professional, polished, and beloved by her team members. The second woman was young, beautiful, and highly confident. She had a smattering of work experience, but nothing lasting more than nine months. She seemed to move from position to position. During her interview, she talked almost nonstop, but didn't ask a single question.

I presented the three candidates to ownership. The woman with the luxury experience was my first choice. The man was my second choice, and the young, attractive woman was my third.

I explained that this was a position that required both gravitas and humility. I shared how the first woman and the man had asked great questions during their interviews. They both possessed maturity and had a history of staying at jobs for years. I explained that the young woman hadn't asked me a single question during our ninety-minute interview. She had talked over me to brag about the things she had done. Her résumé showed that she hadn't stayed at any job for over a year.

The ownership group, made up of six white men, was swift and unanimous in their decision. They wanted the young, attractive woman.

They raved about her enthusiasm. They loved her energy on the Zoom call.

I asked for another meeting to discuss, but they were unwavering in their decision. When it came time to negotiate her salary, the woman asked for $30,000 above what was allotted for the position. She called the Denver Developer directly. He came back to the group with the news that he had approved her salary request.

I knew it was the wrong decision. I also realized that although I was told I had a seat at the table, my opinion did not matter. These men had decided, and there was no room or need for discussion.

I wish I could say that I admired how the young woman demanded her inflated salary and that she rose to the occasion, but the opposite was true. It was immediately apparent that her confidence was covering up her lack of knowledge and experience. Instead of asking for help or admitting what she didn't know, the more she got in over her head, the more stubborn and reticent she became. It was a year before the club was to open, and she had already created an environment of exclusion and judgment.

It came as no surprise to me when we had to let her go eight months before opening day.

We were at a critical time in the launch, and we were down a key player. There was no time to find and train a new membership director.

The Denver Developer called me late one night and asked me what we should do.

I refrained from telling him he should have listened to me in the first place. Because I knew the project, and the job, inside and out, there was only one logical answer. I stepped in as acting membership director through the club opening.

It felt like a huge step backward for my career trajectory. At this stage, I should have been either a highly paid strategic consultant or an equity stake holder in any company I worked with.

Most importantly, it meant breaking the promise I had made to myself to never work for another man again.

The Denver Developer expressed profound gratitude and assured me it would only be for a moment.

I relocated to Denver and spent the next two years working incessantly.

The irony did not escape me. I had tried hard to stop working for men that knew how to be grateful but not fair. I had put myself back in the same dynamic, all over again.

The difference this time was that it was clear from the beginning that I held value. Out of all the employees and owners, I was the only person with membership club experience, and we were opening a membership club. I used this position to speak up more than I ever had.

I worked closely with the Denver Developer. I had a desk in his office. We became friends as well as colleagues. I observed firsthand this man working so hard to better himself. He had business coaches and life coaches and a mentor. He desperately wanted to be a good boss and a good person. He had two young daughters and a wonderful wife, so he had to be aware of the disparity between men and women in the workplace and the world.

Most of all, he knew how essential I was to the success of the project. I worked tirelessly, I was talented, and I had the respect of the staff. I was on the ground, where the other executives were removed and disengaged. I had been hired as a strategic consultant, but instead found myself working eighteen-hour days, seven days a week, to ensure the club opened with enough paying members. Instead of creating strategy, I was taking orders. It is hard to explain how soul crushing it was to go backward at this point in my career, to break the promise I had made to myself.

To compensate for the hasty decision the owners made to hire someone that wasn't qualified, I stepped in to save the day. Once I knew we were going to have a successful opening, I had to find a way to put myself back in the position I deserved.

I gathered my courage and I asked for a seat at the table. A real one.

I scheduled a meeting with the Denver Developer and proposed we create a company to build more clubs like the one in Denver. I suggested that I be the CEO. To me, that title and level of responsibility felt in line with where I was in my career. And it was the correct next step following my efforts in opening our first club.

The Denver Developer told me I didn't *really* want to be a CEO. He said it was a thankless job and would involve too many things that he didn't think I would enjoy having to do. He told me I was excellent at running membership and that everyone already knew how important I was to the success of the club. He convinced me that what I wanted . . . wasn't really what I wanted.

What he failed to realize is that I already knew how important I was to the project. I wasn't looking for acknowledgment and accolades, I was looking for career growth, challenge, and opportunity.

In the Denver Developer's mind, the success of the club should have been enough. But it wasn't.

Crestfallen that he wasn't willing to have a conversation about creating a new company to repeat our success, I asked him what else we could do. Eventually the Developer decided he would create a board, made up of the other stakeholders, and I could be on it.

The board was made up of six men, and me.

The appointment to this board felt like a token gesture on the Developer's part, but I was hopeful that with this seat at the table, I could have a voice and share my vision for the future.

At the end of the year, we had a daylong board meeting. The Denver Developer asked me to prepare the agenda and materials for the meeting. The rest of the board didn't have to do anything but show up. That should have been my first red flag.

I spent weeks putting together an end-of-year review. I was the person on the ground observing the day-to-day operations of the club, so it made sense that I should be responsible for presenting some of the data. The club had seen some great successes, but suffered some noticeable pain points as well. Specifically, our food and beverage program was hemorrhaging money and losing staff left and right. The operating partners, based in Chicago, weren't privy to just how bad things had become. I saw the board meeting as the perfect chance to review our shortcomings and make a plan going forward.

I presented the review. It was thorough and data driven. I had hard facts and member surveys. We looked at revenue and proformas and profit and loss statements.

The next day, the Denver Developer called me into his office and told me we had a problem.

He informed me that my report had upset the other board members.

The Developer informed me I needed to apologize to the operating partners. He told me my report had offended them and they felt disrespected. I was shocked. I had presented the reality of the situation. I hadn't placed blame; I had only encouraged a conversation about how we could reallocate resources and time to help the food and beverage program.

Instead, I was told that I had made waves, bruised egos, and was out of line. And now I had to apologize.

I was told that the owner of the operating partner group, specifically, was deeply offended.

I called this man and we talked about it. Against my better judgment, I apologized.

It turns out that my seat at the table was contingent on not voicing anything that the rest of the table didn't want to hear. I was allowed to prepare agendas, take meeting notes, and celebrate success, but I wasn't allowed to challenge our team or make suggestions for improvements.

In the new year, one more board meeting was scheduled, and then it was radio silence. I was taken off emails and meetings and have no idea if the board continued to meet or just disbanded.

I heard through the grapevine that a major decision to pivot the membership program in a different direction was made without me being consulted at all. My area of expertise, and I wasn't even asked.

I spoke up, and I was iced out.

I felt like my spirit had been broken. I knew it was time to go.

The new membership director was trained and taking over at the club, and I told the Denver Developer I was moving back east.

A few weeks before I left, he received a phone call. It was from the Club Owner I had worked for so many years ago. The Club Owner had been reading about the Denver club and was interested in buying it. On one condition. The Club Owner wanted to talk to me. He said that when he found out I was behind the club, he knew it had to be good.

The Developer asked me to join the call. I couldn't say no. It felt like my past was coming back, and it was either coming to haunt me, or to set me free.

I took the Club Owner through our numbers, our excellent member retention rate, and robust programming. In the end, the food and beverage numbers just didn't add up for the Club Owner. There was too much of a loss there to justify his purchase.

If only we had made the changes I had asked for in that board meeting.

I had known, without a shadow of a doubt, that what I had presented was true and needed to be addressed. But I wasn't heard.

It was disappointing because that sale would have been great for the owners. For me, it would have been a full circle for my career. And perhaps some closure. My seat at the table was a token gesture with no substance or meaning behind it.

I moved back home feeling like all my hard work and all my accomplishments were erased with one swoop of a bruised male ego.

The work experience I should have been the proudest of, and the one I most wanted to see succeed, is instead the one that leaves me feeling the most betrayed.

Dear Denver Developer,

This will be a hard letter for you to read.

You are desperately afraid of confrontation, and I need to confront you.

I am calling your bluff.

I am calling you out on all your work to appear evolved and woke, when in reality, you only ever heard and respected the other white men around you. You never made room or true opportunity for anyone that didn't look exactly like you.

Despite my tireless work and devotion to making your project come to life, you never treated me as a partner or equal.
You expressed your endless gratitude, and you were quick to tell anyone that I was the "secret sauce" to your success, but you never once made that gratitude anything of substance for me.
When I upset the operating partner for sharing our failings regarding the food and beverage program, something you complained about incessantly, I was told I was out of line. I had to call the owner of the company and apologize for hurting his feelings.
Instead of defending me, or even just agreeing that my data and surveys were correct, you said nothing. You let me take the fall for expressing the things that you were too afraid to say.
I took a giant step backward in my career so that your project wouldn't fail.
I made myself available to you any day, at any time of day, to listen to your complaints and worries. I would sit in your office while you rattled off everything that was broken and needed to be fixed. And then I would go fix them.
When I was taking care of everything for you, I was your favorite person.
When I spoke up for myself, I was persona non grata.
Your loyalty, and your love, were entirely contingent on what I was doing for you.
In the end, you couldn't handle my voice in the room.
I believe the reason is simple.
I believe you are afraid of women.
You are only comfortable with a woman if she is constantly feeding your incredibly fragile ego, and if she doesn't make waves.
You talk constantly about your evolved and woke viewpoints. I believe it is because you know you are a fraud, and you are afraid that you could be exposed at any moment.
I want you to think about your daughters. Your incredible, strong, willful daughters.

Would you want some man to feel so threatened by their opinions, their thoughts, and their minds that he feels he must keep any real opportunities from them?
Would you wish for a man to stifle your daughter's passion and vision out of fear that these qualities might expose him as inadequate?
I know you wouldn't. You wouldn't stand for it.
And yet, this is what you did to me.
Rachel

HINDSIGHT

I rewrote this letter a dozen times. I just couldn't get it right. I believe this last version finally starts to hint at what I know was really going on.

I believe that the man in this story was so painfully insecure, and felt so deeply undeserving of his success, that he viewed me as a direct threat to him.

He had to surround himself with other men like him (white, wealthy, born into privilege) to keep the facade going.

Just as in the story with the LA Club Owner, these men fear confrontation because they fear being exposed as frauds.

Unlike many highly successful men, women are seldom given things, nor have they traditionally inherited as much- legacy, position, a company. Many powerful men have been "grandfathered" into their careers.

They often find themselves stepping into another man's (typically their father's) shoes, and perhaps they are plagued with feelings of inadequacy. I believe this gives some men impostor syndrome, and they take it out on those they perceive to be weaker than them. They take it out on women.

What I felt during my experience in Denver was just how close I was to a real opportunity, if only the Developer hadn't been so desperately afraid of me.

Women should not have to compensate, or overcompensate, for a man's insecurities. And yet we do this all the time.

After my two years in Denver, I made myself the same promise I had made before the world went into chaos.

I was done working for men.

ONWARDS

Realize gratitude is not a paycheck.

The Denver Developer was not the first man I worked for that expressed his gratitude to me *every single day*.

And I know he was grateful.

Not only did he tell me every day, but he told everyone else too.

At a certain point, his gratitude grew tiresome. His gratitude wasn't expressed as a check, or a bonus, or a promotion. It was only empty words. And I deserved more.

For a long time, whenever I heard a boss's words of gratitude, I just felt glad to be so appreciated.

I finally realized they were using these words in place of something else: respect. Respect shown through action and opportunity.

This Onwards simply asks you to remember this.

Gratitude is not a paycheck. You can't cash it or put it in your savings account. It's not a cash advance to the top and it won't advance your career. All the gratitude in the world won't pay your rent.

This expression of gratitude from a superior means that they know. They know what you should be given. And they are replacing your advancement with their shallow words.

Imagine that a position opens in your company that you really want, but it is given to a male colleague. On his way past your desk that same day, your boss tells you what an excellent job you are doing, and how grateful he is to have you.

Would you rather have those words, or the new job?

The next time this happens, your answer is simple.

"Thank you. Now about that promotion . . ."

PRESENT DAY, AGAIN

Some amazing things came out of my time in Denver. I was able to save a little money, and I met the love of my life, my fiancée, Jenna.

We moved back to Cape Cod together after our lease was up in Denver.

We thought we would stay for a few months until we figured out where we wanted to settle.

We saw Cape Cod as a pit stop on the way to our next grand adventure.

When my mom received her stage four cancer diagnosis, we stopped looking for other places to be. We are committed to staying here, by her side, while she fights this.

The one thing I know for sure is that my mom can overcome anything. She will be one of those stories you read about. Defying the odds. Mark my words.

I am endlessly grateful, to something much larger than me, that I can be here for my mom.

I can work for myself, taking only the clients that I want and that I can handle.

I am not working on someone else's project, somewhere else.

I am right here. Laser focused on her recovery.

I am also focused on my own healing.

With so much time to write and reflect, I am ready to share my stories, and my journey of speaking the fuck up, in hopes that it will comfort, embolden, and inspire other women.

My last letter is to you.

Dear Reader,

Thank you for taking this journey with me.
This book has been one story after another of times I didn't speak the fuck up.
Thanks to the act of letter writing that I discovered at the beginning of this journey, I come to the end of this book feeling stronger and more confident in my voice than I ever have before.
Writing this book and sharing all the times that I failed to speak up and advocate for myself was depressing and defeating.
Editing this book and examining the common denominators in so many of my stories, was depressing and exhausting.
Did I mention it was depressing?
At many different times in my life and career, I was meek or naive. Other times, I was vulnerable and complicit.
But I am looking at it. I am doing the work. And already, it's worth it.
I feel better and stronger for having gone through it, and now, for having written about it.
That's the power of speaking the fuck up.
It is never too late to say something. To claim something and demand something more for yourself.
The goal of this book is to serve as an example of the importance of speaking the fuck up.
By this point it should be abundantly clear, I made a ton of mistakes. And you might too.
It is a journey, and there is no time frame or guarantee that you will always find your way to your voice.
But when you do speak up, you will feel better, and you will not be alone.
There are more and more of us speaking the fuck up every day.

And this will have a cumulative, earthshaking effect.
It's already started.
We have a hashtag for our Speak the Fuck Up movement: #TogetherweareLouder.
I couldn't have written this book without the two women I love the most in the world: my mother and Jenna. They encouraged me to speak up, every step of the way.
And I couldn't have written this book without you.
I am at my best when I feel like I have something to share that could possibly help another woman thrive.
I was at my strongest and most focused when I was writing this book.
It felt like my life's work because it is.
I hope my message came through.
Now, it's your turn.
Speak the fuck up.
To yourself, to him, to them, in a letter now, or ten years later.
It doesn't matter.
Saying it out loud is what matters.
There will be a bunch of us here to celebrate you when you do.
#TogetherweareLouder.
Yours always,
Rachel

EPILOGUE

Dear Mom,

I know these feel like very dark days.
At night, especially, I am terrified. But I will not show you any of this.
There are so many people that have fought cancer and won.
I know you will be one of these people.
I also know how strong you are. And how strong I am by your side.
Look at all we have done in our life together.
Remember when we absolutely crushed the business you created because you had read about something called the "World Wide Web"?
Remember that year we went to see Prince and Madonna in concert? And when you danced with Paris Hilton at a club in LA and flirted with a famous actor forty years your junior?
Think about the daily walks we take together now. The two of us and our beloved Kussie, the cockapoo. We marvel at everything. It's such a beautiful world, and it's such a beautiful life we have together.
I am so grateful that I can be here by your side as you go through this.
You are, and always will be, what matters most to me.
You are my entire world.
I love you to the moon and back.
Yours forever,
Rachel

Dear Jenna,

From the bottom of my heart. Thank you.
You supported me so much while I was writing this book. You put up with all my bad moods and dark memories. You understood my shortcomings, even though you couldn't really understand what it was like to not speak the fuck up. You have always spoken the fuck up!
You never change who you are to fit a script.
I love that about you.
You are the person I want to go through life with, and to make a family with.
I hope that next year, Mom is well enough that we can try to have the child we have talked so much about, that we have already named.
I know I will give our child a poetic heart. And you will give them strength and courage and an unfailing sense of self. You will make them fearless.
They will be so lucky to have you.
As am I.
Thank you, my love.
Yours forever,
Rachel

To Our Future Child,

Addressing this letter just thrills me. It means that you exist!
I want you to know how loved you are. Your moms and grandmas are so grateful to have you in our lives. You are joining a tribe of strong and resilient women. We will protect you, support you, and inspire you.
We will always be here for you, through all your ups and downs and whatever life throws at you.
I know we will learn a lot from you too.
I can't wait for you to teach us so many things.
If you have made it to the end of this book, you know that I, especially, could use some guidance.
Teach me all the things you inherently know.
Speak as loud as you can, our warrior child.
And dance in the sunshine with us, for all our days.
Yours forever,
Rachel

FINAL THOUGHT

You are now officially a part of the Speak The Fuck Up Movement!

Please check out our site for updates www.speakthe-fuckup.com

And follow us on Instagram @speakthef_up

Finally, we would love to talk to you!

If you would like to schedule a complimentary 15-minute STFU session with Rachel or Jenna, or Rachel and Jenna, you can book time with us on our website.

We would love to hear from you and listen to how you are speaking the fuck up in your own life. And if you aren't speaking up yet, we are here to encourage you.

Remember: You Belong Here and Together We Are Louder.

ACKNOWLEDGEMENTS

This book never would have happened without "the big 3"- My mom, Jenna, and Kussie, my dog. The three of you were constant sources of support, encouragement, and unconditional love.

I am so grateful to Alan Frosh, whose friendship is a gift, and who pointed me in the direction of my publishing team-Michael and Dafna Jenet at Journey Institute Press. I am eternally grateful for their guidance, patience, and wisdom. Michael and Dafna, you have created an invaluable resource for authors.

I am also indebted to all the agents who rejected me. By refusing to take a chance on me, you inspired me to think differently.

To my first readers, David, Alison, Hannah, Aron, Monica, Kara, Celia, Jason, and Kyle, it pains me to think about the state this book was in when you read it, but you told me to keep going anyway. I appreciate you all so much.

To Liesl and Cassandra of 'Strength in the City'. Our first sponsors and just amazing women.

To my favorite Canadians, Tegan and Stephanie, my life is so much better with you in it. Thank you.

To the STFU community!!! Each and every one of you who show up to our events, write a letter, and believe in what we are trying to create.

And finally, to every woman that reads this book and even just thinks about writing her own letter-

I fucking love all of you.

Together we are louder.

About the Author

Rachel Smith is a former corporately dictated, now personally motivated, self-starter and entrepreneur.

Having lived and worked in New York City and Los Angeles for the past three decades, Rachel now divides her time between New York and Cape Cod with her love Jenna, her mom "The Judith" and her dog Kussie.

Rachel aims to empower other women through the telling of her stories and the recounting of the many instances when she didn't Speak the F*ck Up, with the hope that it motivates them to discover and raise their own voices.

Rachel can be found at www.speakthefuckup.com and hosting STFU events around the country.

Speak the F*ck Up is her first book.

Journey Institute Press

Journey Institute Press is a non-profit publishing house created by authors to flip the publishing model for new authors. Created with intention and purpose to provide the highest quality publishing resources available to authors whose stories might otherwise not be told.

JI Press focusses on women, BIPOC, and LGBTQ+ authors without regard to the genre of their work.

As a Publishing House, our goal is to create a supportive, nurturing, and encouraging environment that puts the author above the publisher in the publishing model.

Storytellers Publishing is an Imprint of Journey Institute Press, a Division of 50 in 52 Journey, Inc.

Milton Keynes UK
Ingram Content Group UK Ltd.
UKHW010737210424
441349UK00008B/40/J